For exams in 2022

CW00522394

ICAEW
Tax Compliance

TP06-8-19922-0038

First edition 2013, Tenth edition 2021

ISBN 9781 5097 3892 2

British Library Cataloguing-in-Publication Data

A catalogue record for this publication is available from the British Library

Published by

BPP Learning Media Ltd
BPP House, Aldine Place
142-144 Uxbridge Road
London W12 8AA

www.bpp.com/learningmedia

Printed in the United Kingdom

Your learning materials, published by BPP Learning Media Ltd, are printed on paper obtained from traceable sustainable sources.

Welcome to BPP Learning Media's **Passcards** for ICAEW **Tax Compliance.**

- They **save you time.** Important topics are summarised for you.

- They incorporate **diagrams** to kick start your memory.

- They follow the overall **structure** of the ICAEW Workbook, but BPP Learning Media's ICAEW **Passcards** are not just a condensed book. Each card has been separately designed for clear presentation. Topics are self-contained and can be grasped visually.

- ICAEW **Passcards** are **just the right size** for pockets, briefcases and bags.

- ICAEW **Passcards focus on the exams** you will be facing.

Run through the **Passcards** as often as you can during your final revision period. The day before the exam, try to go through the **Passcards** again! You will then be well on your way to passing your exams.

Good luck!

Contents

Preface

1: Ethics

The topics covered in this chapter are essential knowledge for the whole of your Taxation studies.

They ensure that your advice and communication is appropriate and in keeping with ICAEW's requirements.

Topic List

Fundamental principles

Ethical conflict resolution

Confidentiality and disclosure

Conflicts of interest

New client procedures and tax returns

Regulatory requirements

Disclosure of errors

Anti-money laundering

Tax planning, avoidance and evasion

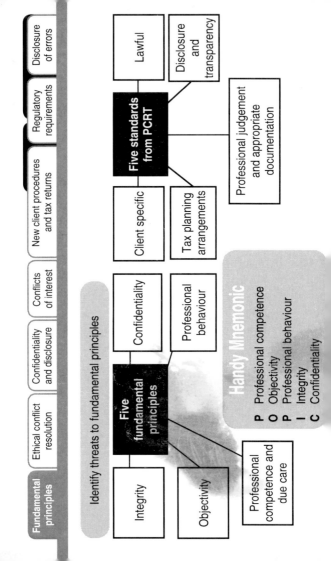

Fundamental principles

| Ethical conflict resolution | Confidentiality and disclosure | Conflicts of interest | New client procedures and tax returns | Regulatory requirements | Disclosure of errors |

Identify threats to fundamental principles

Five fundamental principles

- Integrity
- Objectivity
- Professional competence and due care
- Confidentiality
- Professional behaviour

Handy Mnemonic

- **P** Professional competence
- **O** Objectivity
- **P** Professional behaviour
- **I** Integrity
- **C** Confidentiality

Five standards from PCRT

- Lawful
- Disclosure and transparency
- Professional judgement and appropriate documentation
- Client specific
- Tax planning arrangements

Threats and safeguards framework

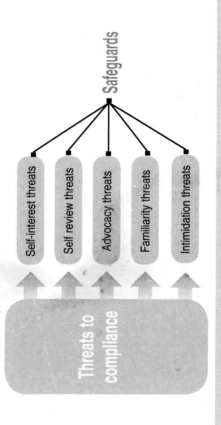

Threats to compliance

- Self-interest threats
- Self review threats
- Advocacy threats
- Familiarity threats
- Intimidation threats

Safeguards

| Fundamental principles | Ethical conflict resolution | Confidentiality and disclosure | Conflicts of interest | New client procedures and tax returns | Regulatory requirements | Disclosure of errors |

Resolving an ethical conflict ■── Whether formal or informal process

Consider:

- Relevant facts
- Relevant parties
- Ethical issues involved
- Fundamental principles related to the matter in question
- Established internal procedures
- Alternative courses of action

Seek internal advice if remains unresolved ──■ Document issue and details

Seek legal advice if necessary ──■ ICAEW confidential ethics helpline

Last resort: withdraw from team or resign

Allowed to disclose confidential information:

1 When **authorised** by the client or employer

2 When **required by law** to do so:

- Production of documents for legal proceedings
- Disclosure to the appropriate public authorities eg, under anti-money laundering legislation

3 When there is a **professional duty** or right to do so

| Fundamental principles | Ethical conflict resolution | Confidentiality and disclosure | Conflicts of interest | New client procedures and tax returns | Regulatory requirements | Disclosure of errors |

Should take reasonable steps to identify circumstances that could pose a conflict of interest.

Conflict situations

Where a firm acts for:

- A client with specific interests conflicting those of firm
- And has financial involvements between client and firm (eg, loan)
- Both husband and wife in a divorce settlement
- A company and its directors in their personal capacity
- Partnership and partners in their personal capacity
- Two competing businesses

Consider:

- Separate engagement teams
- Preventing info access
- Clear guidelines for teams
- Confidentiality agreements
- Regular reviews

Safeguards

- Notify the client of the conflict of interest
- Notify all parties that acting for two or more parties in a conflict matter
- Notify the client that not acting exclusively for any one client
- Obtain consent of the relevant parties to act

Alert! Do not act if one of the five fundamental principles is unacceptably threatened.

Engagement letter

- Set out scope of responsibilities of client and accountant
- Cover every contractual relationship
- Consider including authority to disclose

Client acceptance

- Determine threats to compliance with fundamental principles before accepting
- Apply safeguards to reduce/eliminate

Tax return compliance responsibilities

- Client:
  - Must submit correct and complete returns
  - Decide on disclosure
- Accountant:
  - Acts as agent
  - Not required to audit figures provided
  - Take reasonable care and exercise professional scepticism

Professional indemnity insurance

- Required if ICAEW qualified member in public practice
- Minimum requirement:
  - Gross fee income < £600,000
    - 2.5 times gross fee income
    - Minimum £100,000
  - Otherwise minimum = £1.5 million
- Cover
  - Must remain in place for at least two years after ceases public practice
  - Six years is recommended

Data protection

- If handle personal information the Data Protection Act 2018 sets out legal obligations which include compliance with the General Data Protection Regulation (GDPR)
- Every organisation holding data on EU citizens needs to comply with the General Data Protection Regulation (GDPR) which aims to protect EU citizens from privacy and data breaches
- Compliance with GDPR monitored by Information Commissioner's Office (ICO)
- Public authorities, public bodies and organisations carrying out certain types of processing activities need to appoint a Data Protection Officer (DPO)
- Organisations handling personal data must notify ICO they are data controller and be entered onto register of data controllers. Failure to notify is a strict liability offence.
- Breach of data to be reported within 72 hours
- Tiered fines of up to a maximum of 4% of annual global

Data security

- Passwords should be kept safe and computers physically secure
- Passwords should be changed regularly
- Users should have their own unique log in
- Unusual activity on clients' online HMRC records should be reported immediately
- Suspicious emails apparently from HMRC should be forwarded to HMRC

Procedure

1 Ask client to authorise disclosure of error to HMRC

2 Warn of possible legal consequences of refusal

3 Consider ceasing to act if client does not give consent

Possibly by amending tax return if within time limit

For example, client may face a prosecution under the Theft Act 1968

▶▶ See below

Types of HMRC error

- Legal
- Calculation
- Clerical
- Misunderstanding of facts

Legal considerations

- Deliberate intention to benefit from an HMRC error may be a criminal offence

- If so, it brings the non-disclosure of the error into the scope of anti-money laundering legislation

Anti-money laundering

A number of offences involving proceeds of crime or terrorist funds, including possessing, dealing with, or concealing proceeds of crime including those from tax evasion.

Must register with an appropriate anti-money laundering supervisory authority.

1 Client checking, record keeping and internal suspicion reporting

➡ Appointment of a money laundering reporting officer (MLRO); client checking procedures

2 Not doing or discussing anything that might prejudice an investigation

➡ No word or action that might 'tip off' the money launderers that they are (or may come) under investigation

3 Report suspicions (on reasonable grounds) of money laundering

➡ Report to:
  - MLRO
  - National Crime Agency (use suspicious activity report (SAR))

Consider defences for not reporting ⌐ Watch client confidentiality

Penalties: unlimited fines and imprisonment possible

Tax planning may be uncontroversial or may involve aggressive schemes

Tax avoidance

- Legal method of avoiding/reducing amount of tax due
- No intention of misleading HMRC
- HMRC view:
  - Tax avoidance = bending rules
  - Tax planning = using reliefs as intended
- PCRT uses 'tax planning' for range of legal activities

Failure to prevent the facilitation of tax evasion

If a business fails to prevent its employeesfromfacilitatingtaxevasion thisiscriminaloffencewhichcouldresult inheavyfinesandreputationaldamage due to criminal conviction

Tax evasion

- Illegal way of avoiding/reducing amount of tax due
- Deliberately misleading HMRC eg:

  1 Suppressing information

  2 Providing false information

Case law

Ramsay Ltd v IRC, and other cases:

- Disregard transactions with no commercial purpose
- But not always, eg, where purpose of legislation unclear

  Success of aggressive tax avoidance

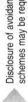

- HMRC can challenge abusive tax avoidance arrangements using the GAAR

- Disclosure of avoidance schemes may be required

2: Income tax computation

The calculation of income tax is key in the Tax Compliance exam.

This chapter first helps you to identify chargeable and exempt income, drawing the taxable items together in the income tax computation.

It also explains how to deal with gifts to charity and tax allowances for married couples.

Topic List

Charge to income tax

Gifts to charity

Interest payments

Married couples and civil partners

Types of income

The main types of income for individuals are:

- Income from employment
- Profits of trades
- Property income
- Interest from banks and building societies   } **Non-savings**
- NS&I saver and investment accounts
- Interest on loans between friends   } **Savings**
- Interest on government securities
- **Dividends**
- Other miscellaneous income

Leave exempt income out of personal tax computation but state exempt

Exempt income

- Interest on NS&I certificates
- Income arising on ISAs
- Betting and lottery winnings
- Premium Bond winnings
- Certain social security benefits
- First £7,500 of rent under rent a room scheme
- Scholarships
- Income tax repayment interest
- Universal credit
- Apprenticeship bursaries paid to care leavers
- Payments from compensation schemes

Income taxed at source

Employment income
- Tax deducted under PAYE system
  - Given **gross** amount in exam, ie, before tax deducted

Income received gross

Received with no tax deducted at source:
- Trading
- Property
- Interest, eg, bank interest, NS&I accounts, government securities, loans between friends
- Dividends

Charge to income tax	Gifts to charity	Interest payments	Married couples and civil partners

Steps for calculating the income tax liability

1 Add all chargeable income together = **'total income'**

2 Deduct reliefs (eg, gifts of assets to charity, qualifying interest payments, property/trading losses) = **'net income'**
- Watch for cap on certain reliefs

3 Deduct personal allowance = **'taxable income'**

£12,570 (2021/22)
- Can tfr £1,260 between BR spouses
- Tapered if income > £100,000

Deduct in this order:
1 Non-savings
2 Savings
3 Dividends

4 Calculate tax at the correct rates on the taxable income
▶▶ See later

5 Add together all the tax at Step 4

6 Deduct tax reductions (eg, marriage allowance, finance costs relating to residential property businesses)

7 Add child benefit charge = **'tax liability'**

1% of child benefit for each £100 of adjusted net income between £50,000 and £60,000

Reduce by tax deducted at source = **'tax payable/repayable'**

Tax rates

1 Non-savings

■ Extend by gross Gift Aid donation and personal pension contribution

❶	BRB	:	20%
❷	HRB	:	40%
❸	Additional	:	45%

2 Savings

■ Only if NS taxable income < £5,000

❶	SRB £5,000	:	0%	
❷	Savings NRB	:	0%	£1,000 – BR
❸	Savings BRB	:	20%	£500 – HR
❹	Savings HRB	:	40%	£0 – AR
❺	Savings additional	:	45%	

3 Dividends

■ £2,000 for all taxpayers

❶	Dividend NRB	:	0%
❷	BR	:	7.5% 8·75%
❸	HR	:	32.5% 33·75%
❹	AR	:	38.1% 39·35%

2: Income tax computation

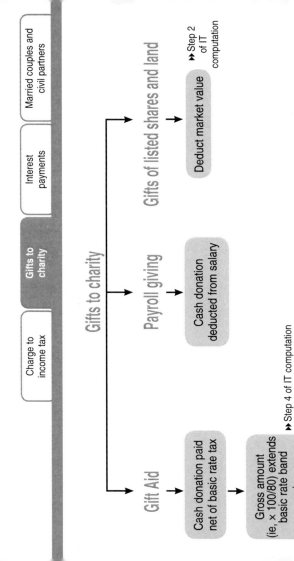

Charge to income tax | Gifts to charity | Interest payments | Married couples and civil partners

Gifts to charity

Gift Aid

Cash donation paid net of basic rate tax

→

Gross amount (ie, × 100/80) extends basic rate band + higher rate limit

►► Step 4 of IT computation

Payroll giving

Cash donation deducted from salary

Gifts of listed shares and land

Deduct market value

►► Step 2 of IT computation

Interest payments

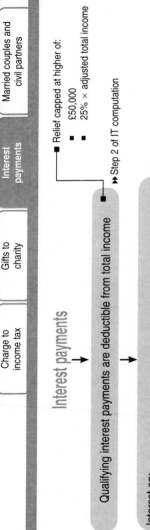

Qualifying interest payments are deductible from total income

- Relief capped at higher of:
  - £50,000
  - 25% × adjusted total income

▶▶ Step 2 of IT computation

Interest on:

- Loans to buy plant and machinery for use in a partnership/employment purposes
- Loan to buy shares in a close company/employee-controlled company (or similar EEA resident co) → Paid gross
- Loan to invest in a partnership
- Loan to pay IHT

Charge to income tax	Gifts to charity	Interest payments	Married couples and civil partners

Independent taxation

Each spouse prepares own income tax computation

Jointly owned assets

1. Spouses share income equally unless dividends from shares in family company

2. Can make declaration to be taxed on income to which actually entitled

3: Property income

This chapter will help you to understand the tax treatment of property income.

Topic List

Property income

Rent a room relief

Property income

Broadly rent from UK property

Computation

Property allowance

- If property receipts ≤ £1,000, the income is not charged to tax
- If property receipts > £1,000, taxed on:

Rental receipts	X
Less rental expenses paid	(X)
Rental income	X

Unless elect:

Rental receipts	X
Less property allowance	(X)
Rental income	X

Cash basis

- Default if property receipts ≤ £150,000 in 12 month period

Rental receipts	X
Less rental expenses paid	(X)
Rental income	X

- Can elect to use accruals basis if desired

Accruals basis

- Used if property receipts > £150,000

Rental income receivable	X
Less rental expenses accrued	(X)
Rental income	X

Relief for finance costs available as a basic rate deduction.

The deduction (Step 6) is 20% of the lower of:

- Finance costs
- Property income
- Adjusted total income

Any finance cost not utilised carried forward to give a basic rate deduction in later years.

Cost of replacement of eg, furniture and furnishings, used solely by tenant, deductible if residential property.

Can take a deduction using approved mileage allowance rather than the actual expenditure incurred.

If take mileage allowance no deduction can be made in respect of other expenditure (eg, CA or running/maintenance costs) and once adopted must use in every future period for that vehicle.

Cannot use if have previously claimed CAs in repect to the vehicle.

Expenses

- Legal and professional costs
- Mortgage and other interest
- Ancillary services, eg, gardening
- Insurance
- Replacement of domestic items
- Repairs and maintenance
- Fixed rate reductions for motor vehicles

Rent a room relief

Rent of up to £7,500 a year on rooms in the landlord's main residence is exempt

Losses

- Net off property losses and profits of same year
- Carry excess forward vs future property profit ← Step 2

Notes

4: Pensions

A single regime applies to all pensions, whether occupational (ie, run by an employer) or personal.

Pension contributions are a tax efficient way of saving for retirement.

Topic List

Pension schemes

Contributing to a pension scheme

Receiving benefits from a pension scheme

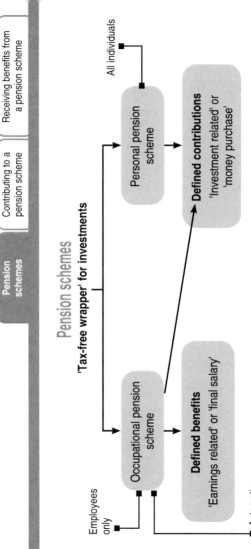

Pension schemes

Contributing to a pension scheme

Receiving benefits from a pension scheme

Pension schemes

'Tax-free wrapper' for investments

All individuals

Personal pension scheme

Defined contributions
'Investment related' or 'money purchase'

Occupational pension scheme

Defined benefits
'Earnings related' or 'final salary'

Employees only

Automatic enrolment

Annual limit

Maximum contribution is higher of:

- Relevant earnings
- £3,600

Annual allowance

- £40,000 (2021/22)

Annual allowance tax charge on contributions in excess of the annual allowance

- Employment income and trading income

Tax relief

1 Personal pension:

- Paid net so automatic 20% tax relief
- Higher rate taxpayers extend basic rate band by gross contributions (ie, x 100/80 – same method as for Gift Aid)
- Additional rate tax payers extend basic rate band and higher rate limit by gross contribution

  ▶▶ Step 4 of IT computation

2 Occupational pension:

- Deduct gross employee contributions directly from earnings to find net earnings (net pay arrangements)

Pension
schemes

**Contributing to a
pension scheme**

Receiving benefits from
a pension scheme

Employer contributions

- Tax free benefit for employee
- Count towards allowances (annual and lifetime) ▶▶ See later
- Usually deductible from trade income for employer

Employers can contribute to either
type of pension
(must automatically enrol staff)

Lifetime allowance

- £1,073,100 = max value for pension fund
- Tested only on **'benefit crystallisation event'**
- If pension exceeds lifetime allowance there are further tax consequences on the excess as the individual draws benefits which can be punitive

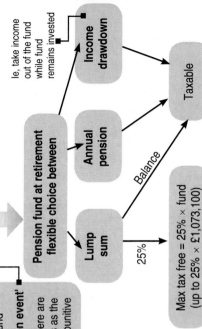

Eg, reach pension age and take pension

Pension fund at retirement flexible choice between

- Lump sum
- Annual pension
- Income drawdown

Ie, take income out of the fund while fund remains invested

25%

Balance

Max tax free = 25% × fund
(up to 25% × £1,073,100)

Taxable

5: Employment income

In this chapter, we review the receipts basis and the main taxable and exempt benefits and then extend your knowledge to include the special receipts rules for directors, further rules on car and fuel benefits, employment related loans, private use of assets and transfers of assets.

We also cover allowable deductions from employment income and the statutory mileage rate scheme.

Topic List

Charge to tax on employment income

Allowable deductions

Statutory mileage rate scheme

Taxable and exempt benefits

Charge to tax on employment income	Allowable deductions	Statutory mileage rate scheme	Taxable and exempt benefits

Employment income

Employees/directors are taxed on income from their employment:

- General earnings
- Specific employment income

— Eg, salary, benefits

Earnings are taxed in the year in which they are received.

The general rule for date of receipt is the earlier of:

- The time payment is made
- The time entitlement to payment arises

Directors are deemed to receive earnings on the earliest of the following:

- The time given by the general rule
- The time the amount is credited in the company's accounting records
- The end of the company's period of account (if the amount has been determined by then)
- When the amount is determined, if this after the end of the company's period of account

General rule

■ Reimbursed expense = exempt if would be allowable as deduction

Expenses must be included as earnings and can only be deducted if they are incurred **wholly, exclusively and necessarily** in performing the duties of employment.

Expenses specifically deductible against earnings:

1 **Qualifying travel expenses** – costs the employee incurs travelling in the performance of his duties and/or travelling to or from a place attended in the performance of duties

■ Normal commuting does not qualify

■ Relief is available for expenses incurred by a site based employee or an employee working at a temporary location on a secondment of 24 months or less.

2 Most **entertaining expenses** unless part of general round sum allowance

3 **Subscriptions** to HMRC approved professional bodies

Round sum allowance

■ Deduction only available if wholly and exclusively incurred for the purpose of **employer's trade**, ie, **not** client entertaining

■ Employer can deduct the **full** allowance

| Charge to tax on employment income | Allowable deductions | **Statutory mileage rate scheme** | Taxable and exempt benefits |

Mileage allowance

Tax free for all employees up to:
45p ≤ 10,000 business miles
25p > 10,000 business miles

- Payments over these amounts – excess is **taxable**
- Payments below these amounts – underpayment is **deductible**

Accommodation

- Annual value of accommodation is a taxable benefit on all employees, unless job related.
- Additional charge if costs more than £75,000

Excess × official rate of interest at the start of the tax year

General rule

- Cost to the employer less amount paid by employee
- Use if no specific rule

Vouchers

- Cost of providing
- Cash/non-cash vouchers
- Credit token (eg, credit cards)

Charge to tax on employment income	Allowable deductions	Statutory mileage rate scheme	Taxable and exempt benefits

Living expenses

Living expenses connected with accommodation (eg, gas bills) are taxable.

- If job related accommodation, the maximum amount taxable is 10% × net earnings
- Furniture available for private use is taxable at 20% × market value when first provided

Cars

The annual taxable benefit for the private use of a car is (list price of car − capital contributions) × %

- Max £5,000
- Reduced by employee contributions
- Time apportioned if available for private use for part of year

- % depends on CO_2 emissions and date of registration. For cars registered before 6.4.2020:
  - 0g/km: **1%**
  - 1g/km to 50g/km: **14%** (unless hybrid where need electric range)
  - over 50g/km: **15%**
- % increases by 1% for each 5g/km over 50g/km threshold up to a **maximum of 37%**
- Additional 4% for all diesels if they do not meet the RDE2 (Euro 6d) standards. Maximum % still 37%.
- For cars registered on/after 6.4.2020 deduct 1% from % given above.

Car fuel

- Fuel for private use is charged as % of base figure (24,600 in 2021/22) 25300
- Same % as car benefit
- No reduction for partial reimbursement by employee

Vans

Unrestricted private use

- 0g/km: £0
- > 0g/km: £3,500 3600

Fuel benefit

- > 0g/km: £669 688

Private use of asset

If an asset is made available for private use, the annual taxable benefit is:

- 20% × MV when asset first provided
- Deduct any employee contributions

Asset transferred

If an asset is given to the employee the taxable benefit is the higher of:
(i) MV when first provided less amounts already taxed
(ii) Market value at date of gift

Less price paid by employee.

Use market value rule only, if asset is:

- Car
- Van
- Bicycle

Loans

Use average or strict method

1. Loans of over £10,000 give rise to taxable benefits equal to the difference between the actual interest and interest at the official rate.

2. A write-off of a loan gives rise to a taxable benefit equal to the amount written off.

Exempt benefits

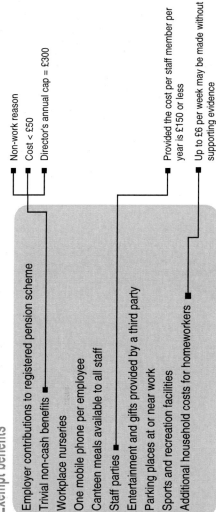

Employer contributions to registered pension scheme

Trivial non-cash benefits —
- Non-work reason
- Cost < £50
- Director's annual cap = £300

Workplace nurseries

One mobile phone per employee

Canteen meals available to all staff

Staff parties — Provided the cost per staff member per year is £150 or less

Entertainment and gifts provided by a third party

Parking places at or near work

Sports and recreation facilities

Additional household costs for homeworkers — Up to £6 per week may be made without supporting evidence

Personal incidental expenses — £5 per night in the UK / £10 per night abroad

Overseas medical insurance

Bicycles provided for cycling to work

Works buses

Provision of vehicle battery charging at or near workplace

Statutory mileage scheme reimbursements

Removal expenses of up to £8,000

Long service awards of up to £50 per year of service — The award must be a non-cash award and the employee must have worked at least 20 years

Eye tests and glasses for VDU users

Health screening assessment or medical checkup

Officially recommended medical treatment for return to work

6: Trading income

You have already met the basics of trading income in the Principles of Taxation exam.

This chapter reviews the basic topics of the badges of trade, adjustment to profits, allowable/disallowable expenditure and basis periods. It then extends your knowledge to enable you to make a full adjustment of profit calculation for a sole trader.

Topic List

Badges of trade

Adjustment of profits

Basis periods

Change of accounting date

Badges of trade

- Profit seeking motive
- Number of transactions
- Nature of the asset
- Existence of similar trading transactions
- Changes to the asset
- Way the sale was carried out
- Source of finance
- Interval of time between purchase and sale
- Method of acquisition

If, on applying the badges of trade, HMRC concludes that a trade is being carried on, the profits are taxable as trading income.

Calculation of trade profits

Trading allowance

- If trading receipts ≤ £1,000, trading profits are nil. (Use receipts accrued/received dependent on whether cash basis is claimed.)

- If trading receipts > £1,000 then use adjustment to profits method unless elect to instead deduct the trading allowance of £1,000.

- Also applies to miscellaneous income such as from a one-off piece of work. (For £1,000 limit add trading and miscellaneous income together.)

Adjustment to profit method

To arrive at taxable trading profits, the net accounts profit must be adjusted.

- Certain items of expenditure are not deductible (ie, not allowable) for trading income purposes and must be added back to the net accounts profit when computing trading profits. Conversely other items are deductible (ie, allowable).

Allowable expenditure

Expenditure incurred **wholly** and **exclusively** for trade purposes.

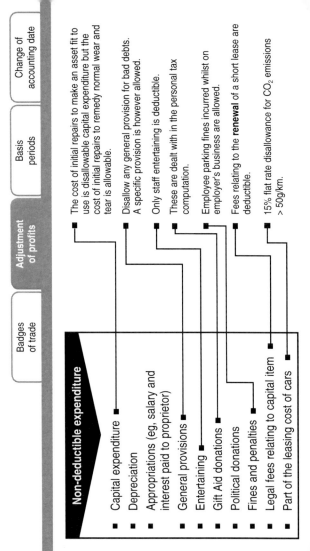

Non-deductible expenditure

- Capital expenditure
- Depreciation
- Appropriations (eg, salary and interest paid to proprietor)
- General provisions
- Entertaining
- Gift Aid donations
- Political donations
- Fines and penalties
- Legal fees relating to capital item
- Part of the leasing cost of cars

The cost of initial repairs to make an asset fit to use is disallowable capital expenditure but the cost of initial repairs to remedy normal wear and tear is allowable.

Disallow any general provision for bad debts. A specific provision is however allowed.

Only staff entertaining is deductible.

These are dealt with in the personal tax computation.

Employee parking fines incurred whilst on employer's business are allowed.

Fees relating to the **renewal** of a short lease are deductible.

15% flat rate disallowance for CO_2 emissions > 50g/km.

Other adjustments

Trading profits not shown in the accounts must be **added**
- Eg, business owner takes goods for own use without reimbursing full market value, or receives payment in non-money form without including money's worth in profits

Non-trading income in the accounts must be **deducted**
- Eg, rental income, profits on the disposal of fixed assets and investment income

Expenditure not shown in the accounts must be **deducted**
- Eg, business expenditure paid personally by the owner

Fixed rate expenses

Certain small businesses can, instead of actual expenses, deduct fixed rate amounts for:

- Motor vehicles
- Use of home for business purposes
- Business premises partly used as home

Pre-trading expenditure

Deductible on first day of trading providing:

- Incurred in the seven years prior to commencement of trade
- Would have been deductible trading expenditure if incurred after trade commenced

Current year basis (CYB)

The basis period for a tax year is normally the period of account ending in the year.

- There are special rules which apply in the opening and closing years of a business.

Any profits taxed twice as a result of these rules = **'overlap profits'**

Relieved when:

- Business ends
- Change of accounting date
  ➤ See later

Opening years

Tax year	Basis period
1	**'Actual basis'**: Date of commencement to following 5 April
2	Depends on length of accounting period ending in year 2: (a) 12 months: tax that 12 months (b) < 12 months: tax the 1st 12 months of trade (c) > 12 months: tax the 12 months up to the accounting date (d) No accounting date ends in year: 6 April – 5 April ('actual' basis)
3	12 months to accounting date ending in year

Closing year ——■—— Tax year that trade ends

■ Basis period for the final year starts at the end of the basis period for the previous year and ends at cessation

■ Any overlap profits not already relieved are deducted from the final year's profits

- If business ends in 1st tax year, tax all the profits
- If business ends in 2nd tax year, tax from 6 April until business ends

Change of accounting date

When a change of accounting date results in:

- One short period of account ending in a tax year, the basis period = the 12 months to the new accounting date

  - This creates additional overlap profits which can be relieved in the normal way.

- One long period of account ending in a tax year, the basis period for that year begins immediately after the end of the basis period for the previous year and ends on the new accounting date

  - To ensure only 12 months of profits are assessed, relief is given for overlap profits that may have previously arisen.

- No period of account ending in a tax year, the basis period = 12 months to the new accounting date

  - This creates additional overlap profits which can be relieved in the normal way.

- Two periods of account ending in a tax year, the basis period starts immediately after the previous basis period and ends on the new accounting date

  - To ensure only 12 months of profits are assessed, relief is given for overlap profits that may have previously arisen.

7: Capital allowances

This chapter reviews the basics of capital allowances on plant and machinery. It then extends your knowledge of this topic by covering aspects such as short and long life assets, hire purchase, business cessations, interaction with VAT, and the structures and buildings allowance.

Topic List

Introduction to capital allowances

The allowances available

Single asset pools

Pre-trading expenditure

Disposals and cessations

Structures and buildings allowance

Capital allowances

Capital allowances = tax depreciation for certain types of capital expenditure on **plant** and **machinery**

Function vs setting test

- Qualifies as plant
- Not plant

Cost and disposal value

- If business is VAT registered:
  - If input VAT recoverable: use VAT-exclusive cost
  - If input VAT irrecoverable: use VAT-inclusive cost
- Asset bought on hire purchase (HP) treated as bought for cash at the date of the HP agreement

Plant

- Office furniture
- Equipment
- Computer software

Machinery

- Machines
- Motor vehicles
- Computers

Purchase of fixtures

Can only claim CAs on fixtures purchased from seller who used them in his trade if:

- Seller claimed FYA or allocated fixtures to pool
  ▸ See later
- Value of fixtures has been fixed (usually by joint election)

Structure or buildings for SBA

Offices, retail and wholesale premises, factories, warehouses, hotels, care homes and structures (excluding land) where the

Main pool

The main pool contains:

All machinery, fixtures, fittings, equipment

- Vans, forklift trucks, lorries, motorcycles
- Cars – CO_2 emissions ≤ 50g/km

Writing down allowances (WDAs)

Balance = **tax written down value (TWDV)**

- 18% per annum on a reducing balance basis
- 18% × months/12 in a period that is not 12 months long
- Can claim lower CAs than maximum possible

First year allowances (FYAs)

- Replace WDAs in period of expenditure
- **Not pro-rated in short/long accounting periods**

100% FYA available for:

- Technologically efficient hand dryers
- **New** low emission cars — CO_2 emissions 0g/km
- **New** zero emission goods vehicles
- Qualifying R&D capital expenditure
- Expenditure by **companies** in a designated enterprise zone
- Electric vehicle charging point

➤➤ See later

Companies (only) are entitled to a super-deduction

Annual Investment Allowance (AIA)

- For all businesses for expenditure up to £1,000,000 pa from 1/1/2019 to 31/12/2021. (£200,000 after this period.)
- For accounting periods straddling 31/12/2021 calculate pro rata. However, max expenditure post 31/12/2021 covered by AIA is £200,000 × n/12 (where n is the no of months post 31/12/2021).
- Scaled up/down for long/short accounting periods
- Allocate AIA to assets eligible for **lowest** rate of WDA — Ie, to special rate pool assets before main pool assets
- Balance of expenditure after AIA receives WDA
- One AIA per group

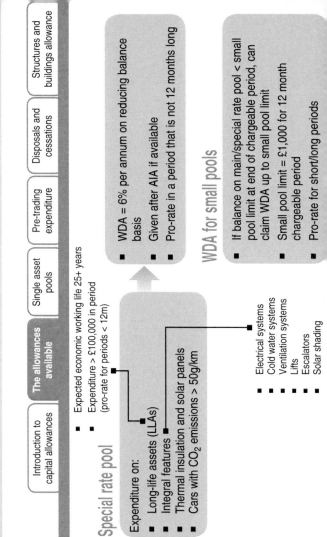

Introduction to capital allowances | The allowances available | Single asset pools | Pre-trading expenditure | Disposals and cessations | Structures and buildings allowance

The allowances available

- Expected economic working life 25+ years
- Expenditure > £100,000 in period (pro-rate for periods < 12m)

Special rate pool

Expenditure on:

- Long-life assets (LLAs)
- Integral features
- Thermal insulation and solar panels
- Cars with CO_2 emissions > 50g/km

  - Electrical systems
  - Cold water systems
  - Ventilation systems
  - Lifts
  - Escalators
  - Solar shading

- WDA = 6% per annum on reducing balance basis
- Given after AIA if available
- Pro-rate in a period that is not 12 months long

WDA for small pools

- If balance on main/special rate pool < small pool limit at end of chargeable period, can claim WDA up to small pool limit
- Small pool limit = £1,000 for 12 month chargeable period
- Pro-rate for short/long periods

Private use assets

— Assets used privately by the owner **not** an employee

- Keep each asset used privately by the business owner in a separate 'pool'
- AIA, FYA and WDA are calculated in full and deducted to calculate TWDV
- BUT can only claim the **business** proportion of allowances

Short life assets (SLA)

Not cars/assets with private use

- An **election** can be made to **depool main pool assets**
- Depooled assets must be disposed of within **eight years** of end of the period of acquisition
- Depooling is useful if balancing allowances are expected

  Otherwise TWDV must be transferred to main pool

Pre-trading expenditure

- Eligible for capital allowances
- Treated as incurred on first day of trading

| Introduction to capital allowances | The allowances available | Single asset pools | Pre-trading expenditure | Disposals and cessations | Structures and buildings allowance |

Balancing adjustments arise

When a column balance becomes negative

- This will be a balancing charge (increases profits)

When a non-pooled asset is sold

- Assets with private use/ short life assets

On cessation to deal with balances remaining after deduction of disposal proceeds

- No WDAs/FYAs/AIAs on cessation

Balancing allowances

Only arise in the main and special rate pools when trade ends

Capital allowances on structures and buildings

Available on new structures and buildings where contract entered into on/after 29/10/18

SBA is % per annum on cost of structure or building excluding land
- Percentage rate 3%
- To be entitled to relief the asset must be brought into use and claimant must have interest in land
- Pro rate if brought into use/sold during the period or if any part used as a dwelling

Sale of structure/building:
- Pro rate SBA for seller and new owner
- Seller has no balancing adjustment and base cost of asset is reduced by SBAs claimed
- New owner takes on 3% of original cost for remainder of 33 1/3-year period

8: Unincorporated trader losses

This chapter introduces the new area of trading losses.

You need to be able to calculate the trading loss available for relief in the opening years of a business.

You must also be able to identify the trading loss relief options for new businesses, businesses that have been trading a while, and those ceasing to trade.

Understanding the restrictions that apply to certain losses is also key.

Topic List

Calculation of loss

Calculate trading income in the normal way. If it is negative then that amount is the loss for the year and taxable trading income is nil.

Alert! Losses in two overlapping basis periods are treated as losses of the earlier tax year only. Do **not** double count the losses.

Example

Sue starts trading on 1.10.20. Her losses are:

y/e 30.9.21   £(50,000)
y/e 30.9.22   £(20,000)

Losses for the tax years are:

2020/21
1.10.20 – 5.4.21   £(25,000)

2021/22
y/e 30.9.21   £(25,000) ie, £(50,000 – 25,000)

First 12 months less the losses allocated to 2020/21

Carry forward (s.83)

A loss not otherwise relieved may be set against the first available profits of the same trade.

Temporary extension of loss carry back in 2020/21 and 2021/22.

Losses may be carried forward for any number of years but if the trade changes, there is no further relief.

Losses **must** be set against the first available profits: they cannot be saved up until it suits the trader to use them.

Relief against general income (s.64)

Relief is against the general income of the tax year of the loss and/or the preceding tax year.

- Partial claims are not allowed: the whole loss must be set off, if there is income to absorb it in the chosen tax year.

- The trade must be carried on on a commercial basis with a view to the realisation of profits.

If claim against general income made can extend the claim to net chargeable gains of the same tax year, less brought forward capital losses.

Temporary extension of loss carry back in 2020/21 and 2021/22.

Loss can be carried back three years on a LIFO basis against profits of the same trade.

Losses offset capped at £2 million for each year (although no

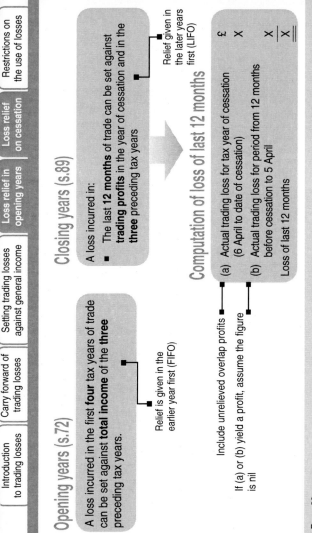

Opening years (s.72)

A loss incurred in the first **four** tax years of trade can be set against **total income** of the **three** preceding tax years.

Relief is given in the earlier year first (FIFO)

Closing years (s.89)

A loss incurred in:

- The last **12 months** of trade can be set against **trading profits** in the year of cessation and in the **three** preceding tax years

Relief given in the later years first (LIFO)

Computation of loss of last 12 months

	£
(a) Actual trading loss for tax year of cessation (6 April to date of cessation)	X
(b) Actual trading loss for period from 12 months before cessation to 5 April	X
Loss of last 12 months	X̲

Include unrelieved overlap profits

If (a) or (b) yield a profit, assume the figure is nil

Summary	s.83	s.64		s.72	s.89
Type of loss relief	CF	CY and/or PY (any order)	Temporary loss carry back extension	Loss in first four tax years	Loss relief on cessation
Set against	Future trading profits from same trade	Total income	Trading profits from same trade	Total income	Trading profits from same trade
Time limits	CF until fully utilised or cease to trade	CY and/or PY	CB to previous three years on LIFO basis	CB to previous three years on FIFO basis	CB to previous three years on LIFO basis
Conditions	■ Automatic ■ Cannot restrict to preserve PA	■ Optional ■ All or nothing ■ Claim in one or both years (any order)	■ Only for losses incurred in 2020/21 or 2021/22 ■ Must have made a CY and/or PY s.64 claim first ■ Losses offset capped at £2 million for each year	■ Optional ■ All or nothing	■ Optional ■ All or nothing
Claim	Agree amount of loss within four years of	Within 12 months from 31 January following	Within 12 months from 31 January following and	Within 12 months from 31 January following	Within four years of end of last tax year in which

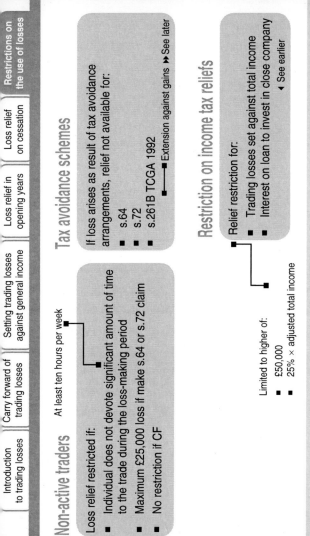

Non-active traders

At least ten hours per week

Loss relief restricted if:

- Individual does not devote significant amount of time to the trade during the loss-making period
- Maximum £25,000 loss if make s.64 or s.72 claim
- No restriction if CF

Tax avoidance schemes

If loss arises as result of tax avoidance arrangements, relief not available for:

- s.64
- s.72
- s.261B TCGA 1992 ➡ Extension against gains ▶ See later

Restriction on income tax reliefs

Relief restriction for:

- Trading losses set against total income
- Interest on loan to invest in close company ◀ See earlier

Limited to higher of:

- £50,000
- 25% × adjusted total income

9: Partnerships

This chapter reviews the basic division of profits between partners and then looks at changes in partnership composition and limited liability partnerships.

Topic List

Partnerships

Limited liability partnerships

Compute trading results for a partnership as a whole in the same way as you would compute the profits for a sole trader (adjusted profit less capital allowances on partnership assets)

- Add back partners' salaries and interest as they are 'drawings'.

Divide results for each period of account between partners

- Remember to pro-rate the annual salary/rate of interest if the period is not 12 months long.

First allocate salaries and interest on capital to the partners, then share the firm's results among the partners according to the profit-sharing ratio (PSR) for the period of account

- If the PSR changes during the period of account remember to split the period of account and allocate the profits according to the PSR in each relevant period.

- When a partner joins, the first period of account for his own business runs from the date of joining to the firm's next accounting date. The normal basis period opening years rules apply to him.

Each partner is taxed as if he were running his own business, and making profits and losses equal to his share of the firm's results for each period of account

- When a partner leaves, the closing year rules apply to him.

- s.64 and s.72 partnership losses restricted in certain circumstances.

Limited liability partnerships

Partners' liability is limited to the amount of capital that they contribute to the partnership.

- Taxed in similar way to regular partnership

- s.64 and s.72 LLP losses restricted in certain circumstances

Salaried members

If partner is classed as 'salaried member', treat as employee for IT, NIC and CT, and not self-employed.

10: Cash basis of accounting

We have seen how to calculate the taxable trading profits for a business using the normal accruals method of accounting.

We now explore the differences for traders using the cash basis. We also remind ourselves that the cash basis can be used in calculating property income.

Topic List

Cash basis for small businesses

Cash basis for property business

Starting the cash basis

Ceasing the cash basis

Interaction with other taxes

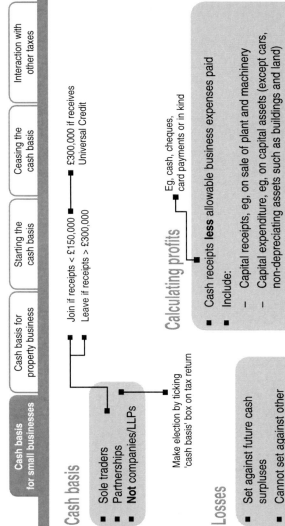

Cash basis for small businesses

| Cash basis for small businesses | Cash basis for property business | Starting the cash basis | Ceasing the cash basis | Interaction with other taxes |

Cash basis

- Sole traders
- Partnerships
- **Not** companies/LLPs

Make election by ticking 'cash basis' box on tax return

- Join if receipts < £150,000
- Leave if receipts > £300,000
- £300,000 if receives Universal Credit

Calculating profits

- Cash receipts **less** allowable business expenses paid
  - Eg, cash, cheques, card payments or in kind
- Include:
  - Capital receipts, eg, on sale of plant and machinery
  - Capital expenditure, eg, on capital assets (except cars, non-depreciating assets such as buildings and land)
  - Loan interest payments made up to £500

Losses

- Set against future cash surpluses
- Cannot set against other income/gains

Cash basis for property business

- Default method of calculating property income for a property business with cash receipts ≤ £150,000, per tax year

Cash receipts	X
Less allowable expenses paid	(X)
Property income	X̲

- Can elect to opt out and use accruals basis if preferred

- Cannot be used if cash receipts > £150,000

| Cash basis for small businesses | Cash basis for property business | Starting the cash basis | Ceasing the cash basis | Interaction with other taxes |

New businesses

Sole trader

- Elect to join immediately
- Stay in scheme until fail to meet criteria or elect to use GAAP

Property business

- If cash receipts do not exceed £150,000 will automatically use cash basis as default unless elect to use accruals.

Existing businesses

Sole trader

- Provided meet criteria, elect to start using cash basis

Property business

- If previously used accruals basis and cash receipts do not exceed £150,000 will automatically move to use cash basis unless elect to opt out.

Adjustments required for:

- **Plant and machinery**
  - Deduction for part of TWDV b/f
  - Not for cars
- **Adjustment expense/income**
  - Adjustment in first year
  - For income/expenditure previously taxed/allowed on accruals basis
  - Opening debtors + opening stock − opening creditors =

Adjustments required on leaving scheme

Plant and machinery

- Unrelieved expenditure allocated to relevant pool
- Eg, HP asset where payments still due under agreement

Adjustment income/expenditure

- Income:
  - Spread over six years
  - Tax as trading income
- Expenses:
  - Deductible in first period after leaves scheme
  - Opening debtors + opening stock − opening creditors = adjustment income/(expense)

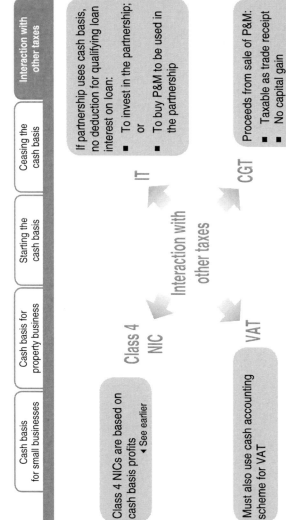

| Cash basis for small businesses | Cash basis for property business | Starting the cash basis | Ceasing the cash basis | Interaction with other taxes |

Interaction with other taxes

Class 4 NIC

Class 4 NICs are based on cash basis profits
◄ See earlier

IT

If partnership uses cash basis, no deduction for qualifying loan interest on loan:

- To invest in the partnership; or
- To buy P&M to be used in the partnership

VAT

Must also use cash accounting scheme for VAT

CGT

Proceeds from sale of P&M:

- Taxable as trade receipt
- No capital gain
  ►► See later

11: Chargeable gains for individuals

This chapter reviews the basic principles of chargeable gains for individuals including chargeable and exempt persons, disposals and assets, how to compute simple gains and the charge to capital gains tax.

It also explains how to deal with part disposals, disposals to connected persons and how to calculate gains on a disposal of shares by individuals which were acquired over a period of time.

Topic List

Chargeable persons, assets and disposals

Computing net chargeable gains

CGT payable by individuals

Married couples/civil partners

Connected persons

Shares and securities

Chargeable persons, assets and disposals

Three elements are needed for a chargeable gain to arise.

1. A **chargeable person**: companies, individuals and partners are chargeable persons.

   → Charities and pension schemes are exempt from CGT

2. A **chargeable asset**: most assets wherever situated in the world are chargeable, but some assets are exempt.

   → Cars
   Gilts
   Medals awarded for valour
   ISA investments

3. A **chargeable disposal**: this includes sales and gifts. Transfer of assets on death is not chargeable.

Computation

Compute a gain as follows:

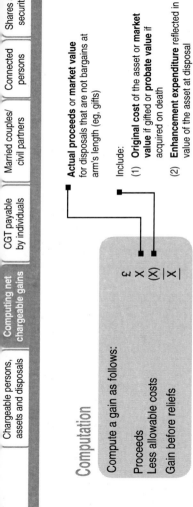

	£
Proceeds	X
Less allowable costs	(X)
Gain before reliefs	X

Actual proceeds or **market value** for disposals that are not bargains at arm's length (eg, gifts)

Include:

(1) **Original cost** of the asset or **market value** if gifted or **probate value** if acquired on death

(2) **Enhancement expenditure** reflected in value of the asset at disposal

(3) **Incidental costs** of **acquisition** and **disposal** (eg, legal fees)

Part disposals

On a part disposal, only take the relevant part of the cost of the asset into account.

$$\text{Cost} \times \frac{A}{A + B}$$

A = MV of part disposed of

B = MV of part kept

Costs relating to the part disposal are deductible in full

Example

X owns land which originally cost £30,000. He sold a quarter interest in the land for £18,000. The incidental costs of disposal were £1,000. The market value of the three-quarter share remaining is estimated to be £36,000. What is the chargeable gain?

	£
Proceeds	18,000
Less $\dfrac{18,000}{18,000 + 36,000} \times 30,000$	(10,000)
Less incidental costs of disposal	(1,000)
	7,000

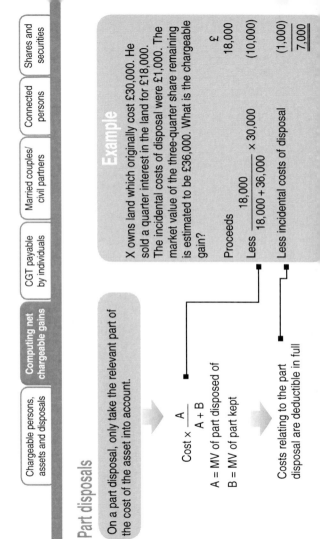

| Chargeable persons, assets and disposals | Computing net chargeable gains | CGT payable by individuals | Married couples/ civil partners | Connected persons | Shares and securities |

Annual exempt amount (AEA)

- **Individuals:** £12,300 (2021/22)
- Deduct after current year capital losses but before b/f capital losses

- Except losses on disposals to connected persons:
  - ▶ See later
  - Set only against gains on transfers to **same** person
  - In same or future years

Capital losses

- Deduct allowable capital losses from chargeable gains in the tax year in which they arise
- Any loss that cannot be set off is carried forward to set against future chargeable gains
- Allowable losses brought forward are set off after the deduction of the annual exempt amount

Example

Zoë made chargeable gains of £14,000 in 2021/22. She had brought forward capital losses of £8,000.

As the AEA is £12,300, brought forward capital losses of £1,700 will be set off in 2021/22. The remaining losses will be carried forward to 22/23.

11: Chargeable gains for individuals

Page 81

Relief for trading losses against gains

Claim to set loss against the general income of:

- The tax year of the loss; and/or
- The preceding tax year

↓

- Can extend the claim for unrelieved part of the loss
- Set against chargeable gains of the same tax year as income tax claim

→

- Available loss is **lower** of:

  - 'Relevant' amount, ie, unrelieved trading loss

  - 'Maximum' amount, ie:

    Ignore AEA for these purposes

	£
CY capital gain	X
Less CY capital losses	(X)
Less capital losses b/f	(X)
Maximum amount	X

Payment of CGT

- Normal due date 31 January following tax year of disposal
- If a disposal of UK residential property, payment on account due within 30 days of completion
- If a gift of land or certain shares, CGT paid in 10 equal annual installments starting on normal due date. (Interest on outstanding balance).

Rates of CGT
Individuals

	Residential property	Other assets
Within BRB	18%	10%
Above BRB	28%	20%

Extend BRB by:

- Gross Gift Aid donations
- Gross personal pension contributions

Business asset disposal ▶▶ See Chapter 12

- Reduces CGT payable on certain **qualifying business disposals**
- Gains qualifying for relief taxed at 10%
- Deduct losses and AEA so taxpayer pays least amount of tax

- Resi prop gains first
- Then other non-BADR gains
- Then BADR gains
- **But** BADR gains use up BRB in priority to non-BADR gains

Spouses/civil partners

Transfers between them take place at no gain/no loss, ie, proceeds = cost.

Connected persons

- Transfers between connected persons (**relatives, business partners, settlor of a trust and its trustees**) take place at market value
  - Losses restricted
  - ◀ See earlier
- Trustees are also connected to anyone connected with the settlor

Matching rules

Disposals are matched with acquisitions in the following order:

- Same day acquisitions
- Acquisitions within the following 30 days on a FIFO basis
- s.104 pool

Computation

Same or next 30 days:

The computation is: proceeds less cost

Special rules apply to shares in the s.104 pool.

Exam focus

Learn the 'matching rules' because a crucial first step to getting a shares question right is to correctly match the shares sold to the original shares purchased.

11: Chargeable gains for individuals

The s.104 pool

The s.104 pool is kept in two columns:

1 The **number** of shares

2 The **cost**

On a disposal of some shares from the pool the cost is calculated on a pro-rata basis.

The computation is: proceeds less cost.

Bonus issues

- Bonus issue shares are free shares
- Treated as acquired at same time as each holding
- Simply add the number of shares to the s.104 pool: there is no cost

Rights issues

- Rights issue shares are purchased at below market value
- Treated as acquired on the same date as original holding
- Simply add the number of shares and cost of the rights shares to the s.104 pool

Alert! Bonus and rights issue shares are only available to existing shareholders.

Value of quoted shares

For CGT value = lower quoted price + ½ (higher quoted price – lower quoted price)

12: Capital gains tax reliefs

In advising businesses of their taxable gains you will be required to identify when rollover relief, gift relief or business asset disposal relief apply.

You also need to be able to calculate the reliefs where specific restrictions apply, for example some non-business use for rollover relief.

In this chapter we also discuss the relief available on the disposal of an individual's private residence.

Topic List

Replacement of business assets (rollover relief)

Gift relief for business assets

Business asset disposal relief

Summary: reliefs involving business assets

Private residence and letting reliefs

Rollover relief

Taxpayers can claim to defer gains arising on the disposal of business assets that are being replaced if both the old and the new assets are on the list of eligible assets.

Eligible assets

- Land and buildings (including parts of buildings) occupied as well as used only for the purposes of the trade
- Fixed (that is, immoveable) plant and machinery
- Goodwill (sole traders and partners only)

The new asset must be bought in the period starting **12 months before** and ending **36 months after** the disposal.

Exam focus

If a question mentions the sale of some business assets and the purchase of others, look out for rollover relief but do not just assume that it is available: the assets might be of the wrong type, eg, moveable plant and machinery.

A depreciating asset is one with an expected life of 60 years or less (eg, fixed plant and machinery).

Is the new asset a **depreciating** asset?
Is the new asset a **non-depreciating** asset?

If a part of the proceeds of the old asset is not reinvested, the gain is chargeable up to the amount not reinvested.

For a **non-depreciating asset** the gain is **deducted from the base cost of the new asset**.

For a **depreciating asset** the **gain is deferred** until it crystallises at a later date.

Non-business use

Relief is proportionately restricted when an asset has not been used for trade purposes throughout its life.

If a non-depreciating qualifying asset is bought before the gain crystallises, the deferred gain may be rolled into the base cost of that asset.

The gain crystallises on the earliest of:

1 The disposal of the replacement asset

2 Ten years after the acquisition of the replacement asset

3 The date the replacement asset ceases to be used in the trade

Gift relief

- Available for outright gifts and sales below market value of **qualifying assets**
  - Chargeable gain is **deferred**

Recipient must be UK resident

Deduct deferred gain from recipient's base cost

Qualifying assets

- Assets used in a trade by donor or donor's personal company
- Shares and securities in trading company
  - Unquoted
  - Quoted: must hold $\geq$ 5% voting rights

Personal companies' restriction:

$$\text{Gain} \times \frac{CBA}{CA}$$

Alert! If any gain remains after gift relief, business asset disposal relief may apply.

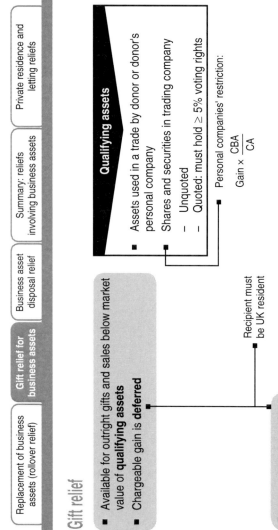

Sales at below MV

Real profit is chargeable ie:

↑ Receive actual proceeds but less than market value

	£
Actual proceeds received	X
Less: actual cost	(X)
Gain chargeable now	X

Rest of gain is deferred by gift relief

Deduct this deferred gain from recipient's base cost

Business asset disposal relief (BADR)

Business asset disposal relief (BADR)
- Reduces CGT payable on certain **qualifying business disposals**
- Lifetime limit: 1 million
- Gains qualifying for relief taxed at 10%

Qualifying period of ownership

- Owned business for two years before disposal
- Owned business for two years before cessation and assets disposed of within three years of cessation
- Qualifying conditions must have applied for two years before disposal

Qualifying business disposal

(1) All/part of a trading business as a going concern (includes partnership interests)

(2) Assets which were used for the purposes of a business which has recently ceased

(3) Shares in the individual's personal trading company in which the individual is an employee

- Owns ≥ 5% of ordinary shares and voting rights
- Where a new share issue dilutes a shareholding to below 5% an election can be made for a notional disposal to be made allowing BADR to be claimed. A further election can then defer this notional disposal's gain until the shares are actually sold in the future

Investors' relief conditions

- No minimum shareholding
- Must not work for the company
- Subscribe for new ordinary shares
- Unlisted trading company
- Shares issued on/after 17.3.16

Interaction of reliefs

If more than one relief available, set off in the following order:

1 Gift relief → Reduces each asset's chargeable gain

2 Business asset disposal relief → Reduces CGT rate

	Rollover relief	Gift relief	Business asset disposal relief
How does it work?	■ Sell asset and acquire replacement ■ Both used in trade ■ Reinvest in 12 months before or 36 months after disposal	■ Gift (or sale at undervalue of) qualifying asset	■ 10% CGT rate applies
What qualifies?	■ Land and buildings ■ Goodwill (not companies) ■ Fixed plant and fixed machinery	■ Business asset ■ Any unquoted trading co shares ■ ≥ 5% quoted trading co shares	■ Unincorporated business sale ■ Sale of shares in trading co if (i) 5% holding and (ii) employee ■ Owned for two years
How much is the relief?	■ Whole gain if all proceeds reinvested ■ Otherwise proceeds not reinvested = chargeable	■ Whole gain if no cash received ■ Otherwise actual proceeds over cost = chargeable ■ CBA/CA restriction for shares	■ Lifetime limit eligible for 10% rate
How is relief given	■ Non-depreciating: gain reduces new asset's base cost ■ Depreciating: gain held over (max ten years)	■ Gain reduces donee's base cost	■ Not a deferral ■ Tax gain at 10%

Private residence relief (PRR)

A gain on the disposal of a private residence is wholly exempt where the owner has occupied the whole residence throughout his period of ownership.

→ Where occupation has been for only part of a period, the proportion of the gain exempted is:

$$\text{Total gain} \times \frac{\text{Period of occupation}}{\text{Total period of ownership}}$$

- No relief for any business use

Periods of deemed occupation

- Absences of up to three years for any reason
- Absences while employed abroad
- Absences of up to four years while employed in UK

⎱ These periods must normally be preceded and followed by a period of actual occupation

- The last 9 months of ownership is always treated as an exempt period of occupation
- Last 36 months is exempt if individual is disabled or in long-term residential care home

Provided that there is no other main residence at the time

Permitted area

The PRR exemption covers a house plus up to half a hectare of grounds. A larger area may be allowed depending on size and character of the house.

Letting exemption

While occupation is shared as part of the property is let out, a gain arising is exempt up to the lowest of:

1. The amount of the PRR exemption
2. The gain in the let period
3. £40,000 (maximum)

Second residence

- An individual is only allowed one private residence at a time. If he has two residences he can elect which one is to qualify
  - Elect within two years of second property being acquired
- Spouses and civil partners must have the same private residence

13: Overseas aspects of income tax and capital gains tax

In this chapter we look at the overseas aspects of income tax and capital gains tax and make sure you understand the meaning of the terms residence and domicile, and their significance.

Topic List

Residence

Determined by statutory residence test:

- UK resident – UK tax on worldwide income
- Non-UK resident – UK tax on UK income

Domicile

- Country of permanent home
- Three main types of domicile:
  - Origin
  - Dependency
  - Choice

UK resident but non-UK domiciled individuals can claim to be taxed on overseas income only when it is **remitted** to the UK

Ie, '**remittance basis**'

Deemed domicile applies if either:

- UK resident for at least 15 or previous 20 tax years. (But not deemed domicile if not UK resident in that tax year nor any tax year from 2017/18 onwards); or
- Born in the UK, UK domicile of origin, and resident in UK that tax year
- Applies for IT and CGT
- Deemed domicile for IHT has different definition

➤➤ See later

Can only change domicile by:

- Severing ties with the old country; and
- Establishing a permanent life in the new country

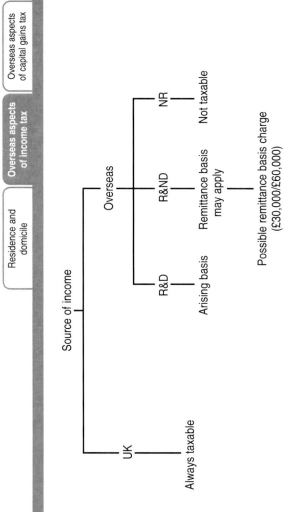

Residence and domicile | **Overseas aspects of income tax** | Overseas aspects of capital gains tax

Source of income

UK — Always taxable

Overseas
- R&D — Arising basis
- R&ND — Remittance basis may apply — Possible remittance basis charge (£30,000/£60,000)
- NR — Not taxable

Employment income

1 Resident and domiciled in UK → Taxable on **worldwide** earnings

2 Resident but not domiciled →
- Taxable on **worldwide** earnings in UK
- **But** may claim **remittance** basis for overseas earnings if employer non-UK resident

3 Not resident in UK →
- UK earnings taxed in UK
- Foreign earnings **not** taxable

Tax free overseas employment expenses

- Overseas board and lodgings
- Any number of visits home
- Travel costs for up to two return visits of spouse and minor children if period of absence at least 60 continuous days

Other income

- **Foreign dividends** – taxed in the same way as UK dividends
- **Overseas interest** – taxed in the same way as UK savings income
- **Overseas trade** – profits calculated as for UK trade
- **Overseas rental income** – taxed in same way as UK rental income

Taxed on **arising** basis unless the **remittance** basis applies, ie, if the individual is not domiciled in the UK

If remittance basis applies, all income, including dividends and interest, is taxed as **non-savings** income

Remittance basis

Income taxed only when brought into the UK

If individual is:

- Non-UK domiciled; and
- Has foreign income

Foreign income taxed on arising basis unless remittance basis claimed.

Remittance basis **automatically** applies if the individual has:

- Unremitted income/gains in tax year < £2,000; or
- No UK gains and UK investment income ≤ £100 which has been taxed in the UK **and** makes no remittances in the tax year **and** either aged < 18 or been resident in UK for not more than 6 years out of last 9.

If remittance basis is **claimed**:

- No personal allowance
- £30,000 RBC if UK resident for ≥ 7 years out of previous 9 tax years **and** aged > 18 years

Increases to:

- £60,000 when resident for ≥ 12 out of previous 14 tax years

Double tax relief is given to prevent income being taxed in both the UK and overseas

1 Agreements

Relief may be given under an agreement between the two countries.

If no agreement:

2 Credit relief

- Foreign income brought into the tax computation gross

- Treated as the **top slice** of individual's income

- Relief = lower of:

  (i) The foreign tax; and
  (ii) The UK tax

- Deduct from the UK tax

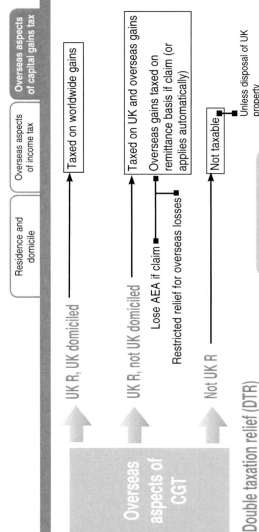

Overseas aspects of CGT

Residence and domicile | Overseas aspects of income tax | **Overseas aspects of capital gains tax**

UK R, UK domiciled → Taxed on worldwide gains

UK R, not UK domiciled → Taxed on UK and overseas gains
- Lose AEA if claim
- Restricted relief for overseas losses
- Overseas gains taxed on remittance basis if claim (or applies automatically)

Not UK R → Not taxable
- Unless disposal of UK property

Double taxation relief (DTR)

Available if gain taxed both in UK and overseas
- Calculated based on sterling figures

→ Relief for lower of UK and overseas tax

14: National insurance and further administrative matters

This chapter reviews the basic principles of National Insurance Contributions (NICs).

It then extends your knowledge to Class 1A and Class 1B contributions payable by employers, NICs on company directors and the principles of annual maximum contributions.

It also deals with an additional self assessment topic – reduction of payments on account.

Topic List

Administration of NICs

Class 1 NIC

Class 1A and Class 1B NIC

Class 2 and Class 4 NIC

Maximum annual contributions

Payments on account

Apprenticeship Levy

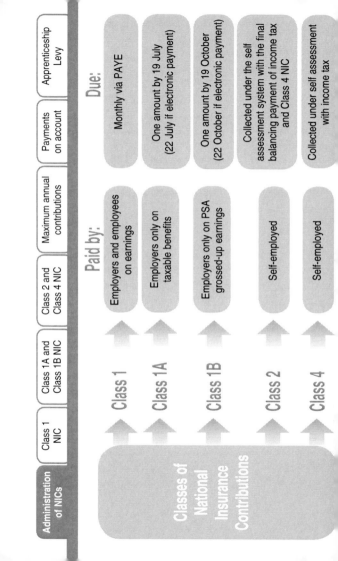

Administration of NICs

| Class 1 NIC | Class 1A and Class 1B NIC | Class 2 and Class 4 NIC | Maximum annual contributions | Payments on account | Apprenticeship Levy |

Classes of National Insurance Contributions

Paid by:

- **Class 1** — Employers and employees on earnings
- **Class 1A** — Employers only on taxable benefits
- **Class 1B** — Employers only on PSA grossed-up earnings
- **Class 2** — Self-employed
- **Class 4** — Self-employed

Due:

- **Class 1** — Monthly via PAYE
- **Class 1A** — One amount by 19 July (22 July if electronic payment)
- **Class 1B** — One amount by 19 October (22 October if electronic payment)
- **Class 2** — Collected under the self assessment system with the final balancing payment of income tax and Class 4 NIC
- **Class 4** — Collected under self assessment with income tax

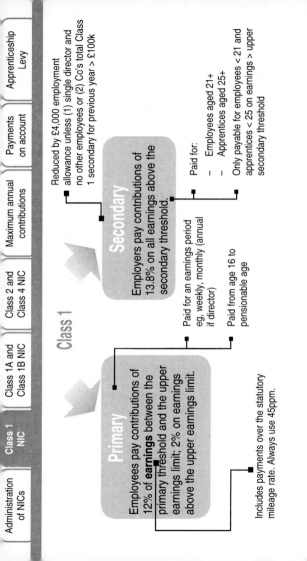

Class 1

Primary

Employees pay contributions of 12% of **earnings** between the primary threshold and the upper earnings limit; 2% on earnings above the upper earnings limit.

- Includes payments over the statutory mileage rate. Always use 45ppm.

- Paid for an earnings period eg, weekly, monthly (annual if director)

- Paid from age 16 to pensionable age

Secondary

Employers pay contributions of 13.8% on all earnings above the secondary threshold.

- Reduced by £4,000 employment allowance unless (1) single director and no other employees or (2) Co's total Class 1 secondary for previous year > £100k

- Paid for:
  - Employees aged 21+
  - Apprentices aged 25+

- Only payable for employees < 21 and apprentices < 25 on earnings > upper secondary threshold

Class 1A

Employers pay Class 1A contributions at 13.8% on most **taxable benefits** provided to their employees.

Class 1B

Payable by employers at 13.8% on the grossed-up value of earnings included in a **PAYE settlement agreement (PSA)**.

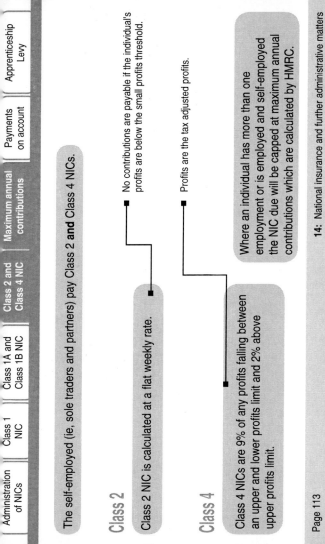

Administration of NICs | Class 1 NIC | Class 1A and Class 1B NIC | Class 2 and Class 4 NIC | Maximum annual contributions | Payments on account | Apprenticeship Levy

The self-employed (ie, sole traders and partners) pay Class 2 and Class 4 NICs.

Class 2 - Class 2 NIC is calculated at a flat weekly rate. - No contributions are payable if the individual's profits are below the small profits threshold.

Class 4 - Class 4 NICs are 9% of any profits falling between an upper and lower profits limit and 2% above upper profits limit. - Profits are the tax adjusted profits.

Where an individual has more than one employment or is employed and self-employed the NIC due will be capped at maximum annual contributions which are calculated by HMRC.

Page 113 / 14: National insurance and further administrative matters

The self-employed (ie, sole traders and partners) pay Class 2 **and** Class 4 NICs.

Class 2

- Class 2 NIC is calculated at a flat weekly rate.
- No contributions are payable if the individual's profits are below the small profits threshold.

Class 4

- Class 4 NICs are 9% of any profits falling between an upper and lower profits limit and 2% above upper profits limit.
- Profits are the tax adjusted profits.

Where an individual has more than one employment or is employed and self-employed the NIC due will be capped at maximum annual contributions which are calculated by HMRC.

14: National insurance and further administrative matters

Payments on account

Interest (but no penalty) due if late

Payments on account (POA) of income tax and Class 4 NICs must be made by 31 January in tax year and by the following July.

Can reduce if lower liability than previous year expected

Each POA is 50% of the previous year's income tax and Class 4 NIC liability less tax suffered at source

No POAs if previous year's tax paid under self-assessment was:

- < £1,000; or
- < 20% of the total income tax and Class 4 liability

Apprenticeship Levy

- Applies to employers with annual pay bill exceeding £3 million
- Levy is 0.5% of the pay bill and is reduced by an annual allowance of £15,000
- Levy paying employers can create an account with HMRC to receive levy funds

15: Inheritance tax – basic principles

This chapter explains how to calculate the value of a transfer for IHT purposes, after deducting available exemptions.

It also shows how to calculate the tax payable on lifetime gifts both when made, and on the death of the donor, taking account of taper relief.

Topic List

Scope of Inheritance Tax (IHT)

Exempt transfers

Lifetime transfers

IHT can only arise if there is a **transfer of value**.

Transfer of value

A gratuitous disposition which results in a reduction of a person's net worth.

Diminution in value

The value of a gift is always the loss to the donor. This is the **diminution in value principle**.

Property outside the UK owned by persons domiciled abroad

Trusts

IHT is often charged when someone (the **settlor**) sets up a trust (or **settlement**) by giving assets to **trustees** to hold on behalf of **beneficiaries**.

Exceptions to the IHT charge

Transfers:

1 Where there is no gratuitous intent;
2 Made in the course of a trade;
3 For family maintenance; or
4 Of excluded property.

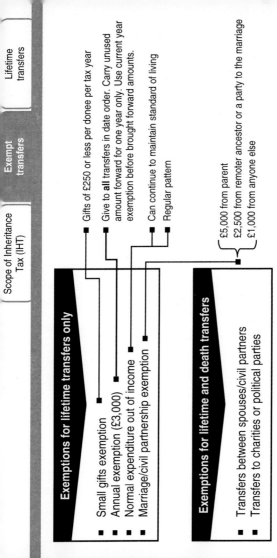

Exemptions for lifetime transfers only

- Small gifts exemption
- Annual exemption (£3,000)
- Normal expenditure out of income
- Marriage/civil partnership exemption

- Gifts of £250 or less per donee per tax year
- Give to **all** transfers in date order. Carry unused amount forward for one year only. Use current year exemption before brought forward amounts.
- Can continue to maintain standard of living
- Regular pattern

- £5,000 from parent
- £2,500 from remoter ancestor or a party to the marriage
- £1,000 from anyone else

Exemptions for lifetime and death transfers

- Transfers between spouses/civil partners
- Transfers to charities or political parties

15: Inheritance tax – basic principles

Lifetime transfers

- **Chargeable lifetime transfer (CLT)**
- **Potentially exempt transfer (PET)** where donor dies within seven years of gift
  ▶▶ See later

CLTs

- Gift to a trust

1 IHT on CLTs in excess of the **nil rate band** is computed at 20% when gift made, with a **grossing-up** fraction of 20/80.

2 Additional IHT if dies within seven years of making gift.

- **Grossing up** is needed if the donor pays the IHT, because he has lost both the amount transferred and the tax.

Exam focus

When you have grossed up a transfer, you can check your figures by computing the tax and the net transfer from the gross transfer.

Nil rate band

IHT charged at 0% on **£325,000** (2021/22)

Additional tax due on death

The IHT on each **lifetime transfer** made in the seven years before death is found as follows:

1 All chargeable transfers (including **PETs** which have become chargeable) in the seven years before the transfer in question use up the nil rate band.

2 Find the tax at full rates (0% and 40%), then deduct any taper relief.

3 Deduct any tax already paid on the transfer (CLTs only – no repayment available).

■ Transfers remain in the cumulation and use the nil band for seven years, then they drop out.

■ A % reduction in the IHT charge is given if the transfer was made more than three years before death.

PETs

■ Gifts between individuals

■ Exempt during donor's lifetime
■ Fully exempt if survives seven years from gift
■ IHT if dies within seven years of making gift

15: Inheritance tax – basic principles

Fall in value relief

If at date of donor's death a gifted asset has either:

1 Been sold for less than its MV when originally gifted

or

2 Is still held but is worth less than its MV when originally gifted

Deduct 'fall in value' from gross chargeable transfer (GCT)

Alert! Fall in value relief only affects the calculation of tax for the donee. It does **not** affect the donor's cumulative total.

16: Inheritance tax – death estate and valuation

This chapter deals with the IHT payable on an individual's death estate after taking account of reliefs and exemptions and using the special valuation rules for certain assets.

Topic List

IHT on the death estate	Residence nil rate band	Transfer of nil rate bands	Reduced death tax rate	Valuation

Death estate

The death estate includes all assets owned at death

Debts

Debts ── Eg, accrued rent payable to date of death, outstanding loans, etc

- Deduct debt from asset debt relates to, eg, mortgage is deducted from the property it was taken out on

- Only deduct if remains unpaid for commercial reason and not to obtain a tax advantage

- No deduction if debt incurred to acquire 'excluded property' ── Ie, foreign assets of non-doms

Other liabilities

Can deduct:

- Taxes to date of death
- Reasonable funeral expenses ── Including tombstone

Calculating death tax

1 Calculate total value of estate (probate value less liabilities) —————— Market value at date of death

2 Deduct any residence nil rate band – ▸▸ See later

3 Nil rate band is used by chargeable transfers in last seven years
Remaining nil band at 0%
- CLTs and PETs that have become chargeable
- Increase nil rate band by proportion equal to unused proportion of nil rate band of deceased spouse(s)/civil partner(s) up to a maximum of 100%

4 Balance of estate at 40% (36% if 10% or more of net estate given to charity)
Deduct quick succession relief (QSR) ▸▸ See below

16: Inheritance tax – death estate and valuation

Quick succession relief (QSR)

QSR is given when someone dies within five years of receiving property in a chargeable transfer (the first transfer).

QSR is deducted from the IHT on the estate.

Period between transfers	% relief
1 year or less	100
1–2 years	80
2–3 years	60
3–4 years	40
4–5 years	20
> 5 years	0

Computation

1 Take the tax paid on the first transfer, and multiply it by the net transfer/the gross transfer

2 Then multiply the result by a percentage, from 100% (for a gap of one year or less) to 20% (for a gap of more than four years)

Residence nil rate band available if they:

- Die on/after 6 April 2017
- Own home included in death estate
- Left to direct descendant(s)

Withdrawn by £1 for every £2 where estate exceeds £2 million

Lower of:

- Value of home to direct descendants
- Max threshold (£175,000 in 2021/22)

Deduct from chargeable estate before deducting remaining basic nil rate band

| IHT on the death estate | Residence nil rate band | **Transfer of nil rate bands** | Reduced death tax rate | Valuation |

Transfer of nil rate bands

Unused % of deceased spouse/civil partner's unused nil rate band can be passed to surviving spouse/civil partner.

Where surviving spouse/civil partner dies after 5 April 2017 any percentage of unused residence nil rate band can be transferred.

A claim is made by personal representative on death of surviving spouse/civil partner usually within two years from end of month of death.

Reduced rate of IHT of 36% applies if 10% or more of net chargeable estate left to charity.

'Net chargeable estate' is value of estate after deducting reliefs, exemptions and available nil rate band but before deducting residence nil rate band and the charitable legacy itself.

| IHT on the death estate | Residence nil rate band | Transfer of nil rate bands | Reduced death tax rate | **Valuation** |

Valuation

Assets are generally valued at their open market values.

Diminution in value

Value before transfer	X
Value left with after transfer	(X)
Transfer of value	X

Related property

Related property includes:

1 Property owned by the transferor's spouse

2 Property which the transferor or his spouse gave to a charity or political party in an exempt transfer, if the recipient has owned the property within the preceding five years

Value at the higher of:

- Value ignoring the related property
- Value including the related property

Special valuation rules

1. Value quoted shares and securities at the lower of:
   - The quarter up basis
   - The average of the highest and lowest marked bargains

   → HMRC's Shares and Assets Valuation Office values unquoted shares

2. Value unit trusts at the bid price (the lower price).

3. Value of life insurance depends on whose death policy will pay out:
   - Deceased   –   Maturity proceeds
   - Someone else –   Open market value

   → If written 'in trust' the policy is completely outside the deceased's estate

4. Land jointly owned
   - Related property   –   No deduction
   - Not related property   –   5%–15% deduction

17: Inheritance tax – reliefs and other aspects

This chapter deals with business property relief, the overseas aspects of IHT, the administration provisions for IHT and the interaction of IHT and CGT.

Topic List

Business property relief

Overseas aspects of IHT

Administration of IHT

Interaction of IHT and CGT

Business property relief

BPR applies on lifetime and death transfers. It reduces the value transferred.

R elevant business property

BPR applies to transfers of:

1. Businesses
2. Unquoted securities where the transferor has control of the company
3. Unquoted shares (includes AIM listed shares)
4. Quoted shares or securities which gave the transferor control of the company
5. Land and buildings and plant and machinery used by the individual donor's partnership or company he controls

- Businesses of holding or dealing in financial investments or land are excluded
- 100% relief ■—■ Watch for excepted assets
- 50% relief
  - Can combine certain shorter periods, eg, if received on death of spouse

O wnership

The transferor must usually have owned the property for two years.

S ale contract

There must not be a binding contract for sale at date of transfer.

E xcepted assets

No relief for assets not used/needed in the business. ■—■ Exclude investment assets/surplus cash

Withdrawal of BPR

For **lifetime transfers**, BPR does not apply when computing the tax on death within seven years of the transfer if:

1 The donee has sold/gifted the property before the donor's death

— Unless full proceeds of sale used to buy qualifying replacement property

2 The donee still owns the property but is not using it for business purposes

3 The property is no longer relevant business property

— Eg, unquoted shares have become quoted (and the donee does not control the company)

- UK domiciled – IHT on all assets wherever situated
- Non-UK domiciled – IHT only on UK assets

Deemed domicile

Treat as UK domiciled for IHT purposes only if:

- Domiciled in the UK under general law at any time in the three previous years;
- A 'formerly domiciled resident'; or
- Resident in the UK for at least 15 of the previous 20 years and including at least one of the four tax years ending with the current tax year.

Double tax relief

DTR is available if property is situated overseas and suffers a foreign equivalent of IHT.

- DTR is the lower of the UK IHT on the asset (at the average rate) and the foreign tax
- The DTR is deducted from the IHT

Location of assets

- Immovable property – where situated
- Debts – where debtor resident
- Registered shares – where registered
- Life policies – where proceeds are payable
- Bank account – where branch situated
- Goodwill – where business carried on

Transfers between spouses/civil partners

- Both UK domiciled: Completely exempt
- To non-UK domiciled spouse/CP: Exemption **limited** to value of nil rate band

Applies for IHT only
(not IT or CGT)

UK domicile election

- Non-UK domiciled spouse/CP can make a UK domicile election
- Spouse exemption = unlimited
- But brings all overseas assets within scope of UK IHT

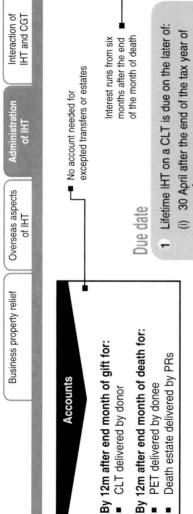

Accounts

By 12m after end month of gift for:
- CLT delivered by donor

By 12m after end month of death for:
- PET delivered by donee
- Death estate delivered by PRs

- No account needed for excepted transfers or estates

Interest runs from six months after the end of the month of death

Due date

1 Lifetime IHT on a CLT is due on the later of:
  (i) 30 April after the end of the tax year of transfer
  (ii) Six months after the end of the month of transfer

2 IHT due on CLTs/PETs as a result of death is due six months after end of the month of death.

3 The due date for IHT on the death estate is the date of delivery of the account.

Instalment payments

- Land and buildings
- Most unquoted shares and securities
- Business/interest in business

- IHT on certain property can be paid in ten equal annual instalments on CLTs where tax is borne by the donee, or on the death estate.

- Additionally, IHT due on PETs as a result of the death of the donor can be paid in instalments.

Penalties

For an account submitted late:

- Immediate fixed penalty — Max £100
- Daily penalties — Up to £60 per day
- > 6m < 12m — Additional max £100
- > 12m — Additional max £3,000

Based on:
- Amount of tax
- Period account outstanding

17: Inheritance tax – reliefs and other aspects

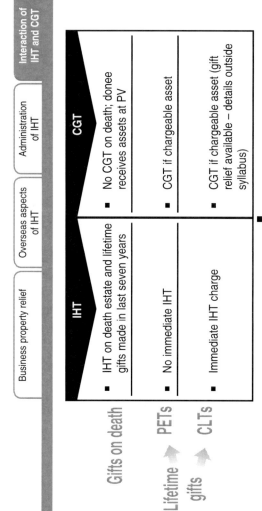

Interaction of IHT and CGT

	IHT	CGT
Gifts on death	■ IHT on death estate and lifetime gifts made in last seven years	■ No CGT on death; donee receives assets at PV
Lifetime gifts → PETs	■ No immediate IHT	■ CGT if chargeable asset
Lifetime gifts → CLTs	■ Immediate IHT charge	■ CGT if chargeable asset (gift relief available – details outside syllabus)

Gifts to spouse/civil partner on death or during lifetime – no IHT or CGT

Top navigation tabs: Business property relief | Overseas aspects of IHT | Administration of IHT | Interaction of IHT and CGT

18: Corporation tax

This chapter builds on your basic knowledge of corporation tax by covering computation of taxable total profits for long periods of account.

It then considers specific administrative matters for companies including corporation tax instalments, particularly for a short accounting period.

Topic List

Charge to corporation tax

Taxable total profits and computation of corporation tax

Administration of corporation tax

| Charge to corporation tax | Taxable total profits and computation of corporation tax | Administration of corporation tax |

Residence

A UK resident company is chargeable on its worldwide profits. A company is resident in the UK if it is incorporated in the UK or if its central management and control are in the UK.

Alert! An accounting period can never be > 12 months.

If a company prepares accounts for a longer period, it must be split into two CT accounting periods.

First 12 months form the first accounting period

Remaining months form the second accounting period

Period of account

A period of account is the period for which accounts are prepared.

Accounting period

An accounting period is the period for which corporation tax is charged.

- Begins when the company starts to trade, acquires a source of income or immediately after the end of the previous accounting period

- Ends 12 months after it starts, when the period of account ends, when it starts or ceases to trade or when it ceases to be UK resident

Taxable total profits

A company's **taxable total profits** are arrived at by adding together its various sources of income and chargeable gains and then deducting qualifying donations.

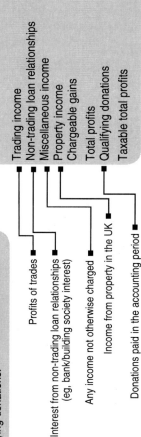

Proforma for calculating taxable total profits

	£
Trading income	X
Non-trading loan relationships	X
Miscellaneous income	X
Property income	X
Chargeable gains	X
Total profits	X
Qualifying donations	(X)
Taxable total profits	X

- Profits of trades
- Interest from non-trading loan relationships (eg, bank/building society interest)
- Any income not otherwise charged
- Income from property in the UK
- Donations paid in the accounting period

Alert! Exempt dividends from other UK and overseas companies are not included in taxable total profits.

Certain items of expenditure are **allowable** (ie, can be deducted) when calculating trading profits.

Deductible expenditure

- Incurred **wholly** and **exclusively** for trade purposes
- Gifts to customers not costing > £50 per donee per year and marked with business name (but not food, drink, tobacco or vouchers for goods)
- Interest on trade related borrowings
- Cost of registering patents and trademarks
- Trade related patent royalties
- Legal fees for renewing a **short** lease (≤ 50 years)
- Trade subscriptions and **small** donations to **local** charities
- Most employee termination payments made for purposes of trade, where trade is continuing
- Payments to registered pension schemes

  - Deductible when paid

Capital allowances

- In addition to the usual capital allowances, companies are entitled to temporary first year allowances when incurring qualifying expenditure on new assets (except cars) between 1 April 2021 and 31 March 2023.
- A 130% super-deduction is available for main pool plant and machinery with a 50% special rate allowance for special rate pool assets.
- The super-deduction will be preferable for main pool items but the AIA will be preferred for special rate pool assets.
- On a disposal of an asset on which these first year allowances have been claimed there will be a balancing charge equal to proceeds × 1.3 (for super-deduction assets) or proceeds × 50% (for special rate allowance assets).

For a long period of account, divide profits between the accounting periods as follows:

Division of profits		
	Trading income	Time apportion amount before CAs
	CAs	Compute separately for each period
	Property income	Time apportionment
	NTLR	Accruals basis
	Miscellaneous income	Time apportion
	Gains	Allocate to period of disposal
	Qualifying donations	Allocate to period in which paid

Corporation tax rate

Rate of corporation tax (CT) is set for financial years.

A financial year runs from 1 April in one year to 31 March in the next. **Financial year 2021 (FY 2021) runs from 1 April 2021 to 31 March 2022.**

19% for FY20 and FY21

Returns

A company must normally file its CT return (CT600) by the due filing date which is the later of:

- 12 months after the end of the period to which the return relates

- 3 months after a notice requiring the return was issued

Payment

➤ See below

Has 'augmented profits' > £1.5m

'Large' companies must pay their anticipated CT liability in quarterly instalments.

'Very large' companies (AP > £20m) pay their instalments 4 months earlier than normal

Due 14th of the month

Late filing penalties

Fixed penalties

- £100 ≤ 3m late (£500 if 3rd consecutive late return)
- £200 > 3m late (£1,000 if 3rd consecutive late return)

Tax-geared penalties

- > 18 < 24m – 10% × tax outstanding at 18m from end of return period

- ≥ 24m – 20% × tax outstanding at 18m from end of return period

12 month AP:

Instalments due in:

- Months 7 and 10 of the period
- Months 1 and 4 of the following period

AP < 12 (n) months:

- Each instalment = $3 \times CT/n$
- Instalments due at 3 monthly intervals
- Final instalment in month 4 of the following period

18: Corporation tax

Augmented profits (AP)

Taxable total profits plus exempt ABGH distributions

UK and overseas dividends from non-51% subsidiaries

- Multiply by months/12 for short accounting periods
- Divide by number of **related 51% group companies** (plus this co) at the end of the previous accounting period

≤ £1.5m

Payment due date is nine months and 1 day after the end of the accounting period.

> £1.5m

Large company so payment due in instalments unless:

- CT liability < £10,000; or
- Not large in PY, and APs ≤ £10m.

Example

A Ltd, which has one related 51% group company at 30.6.21, prepares accounts for the nine months to 31.3.22. The limit for this period is:

$$9/12 \times \frac{1,500,000}{2}$$

$$= £562,500$$

Related 51% group company

- Include 51% subsidiaries (directly or indirectly own > 50%)
- Ignore passive companies

Business payment support service

- Helps businesses unable to meet tax payments
- Allows temporary options to spread tax payments over time

19: Chargeable gains for companies

This chapter deals with calculating chargeable gains for companies.

A key area is the rules for the disposal of shares and securities, including recognising when an exemption applies.

Topic List

Computing chargeable gains for companies

Disposal of shares and securities

Bonus and rights issues

Substantial shareholding exemption

Non-resident companies and chargeable gains

Computing chargeable gains for companies	Disposal of shares and securities	Bonus and rights issues	Substantial shareholding exemption	Non-resident companies and chargeable gains

Computation

Compute a gain as follows:

	£
Proceeds	X
Less: allowable costs	(X)
indexation allowance	(X)
Chargeable gain	X

(1) Cannot create or increase a loss

(2) Round to three decimal places (or zero if negative) before multiplying by cost

(3) Frozen at December 2017

$$\frac{\text{RPI for December 2017 (or month of disposal if earlier)} - \text{RPI for month of acquisition}}{\text{RPI for month of acquisition}}$$

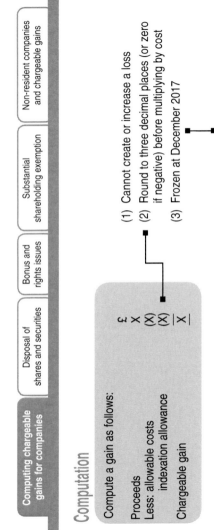

No IA for these shares

Matching rules for shares

Disposals are matched with acquisitions in the following order:

- Same day acquisitions
- Acquisitions within the previous nine days (FIFO basis)
- s.104 pool (pool runs from 1.4.82)

The s.104 pool

The s.104 pool is kept in three columns:

1 The **number** of shares

2 The **cost**

3 The **indexed cost**

- On a disposal of some shares from the pool, the cost and indexed cost are calculated on a pro-rata basis.

- The computation is: proceeds less cost less IA.

- The IA is the excess of the indexed cost over the cost. It cannot increase or create a loss.

- The indexation factor in this pool is **not** rounded to three decimal places.

- Final indexation up to December 2017 when indexation frozen

Bonus issues

- Bonus issue shares are free shares
- Treated as acquired at same time as each holding
- Simply add the number of shares to each holding as there is no cost to add

Rights issues

- Rights issue shares are purchased at below market value
- Treated as acquired at same time as each holding
- Add the number of shares and cost of the rights shares to each holding
- Index s.104 pool to date of the rights issue (unless rights issue after December 2017 when indexation frozen)

Alert! Bonus and rights issue shares are only available to existing shareholders.

Substantial shareholding exemption

1. A company owns 10% or more in another trading company

2. For 12 months over a six-year period

3. Gain on sale of shares is exempt (loss is not allowable)

Non-resident companies and chargeable gains

1. On a disposal by a non-resident company of a UK non-residential property or asset deriving at least 75% of its value from UK land only the gain from 6 April 2019 is taxable.

   – Use 'cost' based on MV at 5/4/19; or
   – Elect to tax whole gain/loss.

2. On a disposal by a non-resident company of UK residential property the gain from 6/4/15 is taxable.

   – Use 'cost' based on MV at 5/4/15;
   – Elect to time apportion and use only post 4/15 gain; or
   – Elect to use full gain or loss based on original cost.

3. Corporation tax due on these disposals will be within 30 days of completion of disposal.

20: Additional aspects of corporation tax

This chapter deals with the treatment of large pension contributions to employees' pensions, loan relationships, intangible assets owned by a company, research and development (R&D) expenditure, the taxation of property income and double tax relief.

Topic List

Pension contributions

Loan relationships

Intangible fixed assets

Research and development expenditure

Property income

Double taxation relief

Pension contributions	Loan relationships	Intangible fixed assets	Research and development expenditure	Property income	Double taxation relief

Loan relationships

A company that borrows or invests money has a loan relationship.

Non-trading loan relationship

- Held for non-trade purposes (eg, bank account held for investment purposes)
- Tax income (eg, interest income) and capital profit accruing on non-trading loan relationships
- Deduct expenses accruing from the pool of interest income

Net loss (non-trading deficit) can be relieved
▶▶ See Chapter 21

Employer pension contributions

- Contributions paid by employer are allowable trading expense in period **paid**

Trading loan relationship

- Loan for trade purposes (eg, debentures issued to raise money to buy plant and machinery)
- Costs (eg, interest) accruing are deductible trade expenses

Exam focus

Interest income is never treated as trading profit in the exam.

Intangible fixed assets

■ Eg, patents, copyrights, goodwill

Income/expenditure dealt with as trading income in accounts. No adjustment required if accounts properly prepared (except for goodwill).

Income:
Eg, profit on disposal of IFA, royalty income

Expenditure:
Eg, royalty payable, loss on disposal of IFA, amortisation (but goodwill amortisation not allowable)

20: Additional aspects of corporation tax

Pension contributions | Loan relationships | Intangible fixed assets | **Research and development expenditure** | Property income | Double taxation relief

Research and development

Tax deduction

100% FYA for capital expenditure (although if P&M qualifying for super-deduction the s-d is preferable) (Chapter 7)

Additional relief for qualifying revenue research and development

Qualifying expenditure staff costs, consumables and software

Additional deduction for 130% × qualifying expenditure if SME

R&D expenditure credit (RDEC) available for large companies
13% × qualifying R&D expenditure:

- Added as 'above the line' tax credit to trading income; and
- Deducted from corporation tax liability

Property income – income from land and buildings

- Mainly use same rules as for an individual, however, companies must use the accruals basis ◄◄ See Chapter 3

- Losses can, however, be set against total profits and not just other property income

Mortgage interest

- Treatment is different from an individual

- Deductible under the loan relationship rules, **not** as a property business expense

Double taxation relief

- Unilateral relief where UK and foreign taxes suffered on same income and no Double Tax Treaty.

- Maximum relief lower of:
  - UK tax on foreign income; and
  - Foreign tax suffered.

Eg. withholding tax

Offsetting deductions

Eg, qualifying charitable donations, trading losses

Set against:

- UK income first; then
- Foreign income with lowest marginal overseas tax rate.

Example

A UK company receives overseas rental income of £80,000 net of 15% withholding tax. The company's only other income in the year to 31 March 2022 is trading income of £2,000,000.

The taxable overseas income is:

£80,000 × $^{100}/_{85}$ = £94,118

The UK tax payable is:

£94,118 × 19% = £17,882 less DTR of £14,118 (as this is lower than the UK tax).

21: Corporation tax losses

This chapter introduces you to corporation tax losses.

You will be expected to be able to calculate the loss relief available for a company's trading and non-trading losses.

You must also be able to calculate the taxable total profits after the losses are relieved.

Topic List

Introduction to company losses

Carry forward of losses

Setting losses against total profits

Non-trading loan relationship deficits

Restriction on carried forward relief

Property losses

- Automatically set off against total profits of the same AP
- Excess losses can be:
  - CF as a property loss of the following period
  - A claim determines the amount of loss to be offset against total profits (subject to restriction if loss is large) ▸▸ See later
  - Group relieved

Capital losses

- Can only be set against chargeable gains in current or future accounting periods
- Must be set against the first available gains
- Amount relieved on carry forward may be restricted if loss is large ▸▸ See later

Non-trading loan relationship deficit

Set off in similar way to trading losses ▸▸ See later

Trading losses

A company's trading loss may be:

(1) Set against other profits of the **same** accounting period (s.37).

(2) Set against profits of the **previous 12 months** (s.37).

(3) Carried forward to set against the total profits of the following accounting period (s.45A).

- If claiming relief (2), must claim relief (1) first
- Both are all or nothing claims
- When carrying forward the loss under (3) a **claim** must be made within two years of the accounting period in which the loss is offset to **specify** the amount of relief. Any loss remaining unused can be carried forward again (or group relieved)

Terminal loss relief (s.37)

12-month CB period extended to 36 months where trading loss arose in 12 months before trade ceases.

Before QCDs but after relief for a non-trading loan relationship deficit

If pro-rating is necessary, pro-rate profits before QCDs to compute maximum relief

Temporary extended loss carry-back

For AP ending between 1/4/20 and 31/3/22 the usual carry back against total profits is extended to the preceding three years on a LIFO basis.

Maximum losses carried back capped at £2 million for AP ending 1/4/20–31/3/21 and a separate £2 million for AP ending 1/4/21–31/3/22.

Restriction of carried forward relief ➤➤ See later

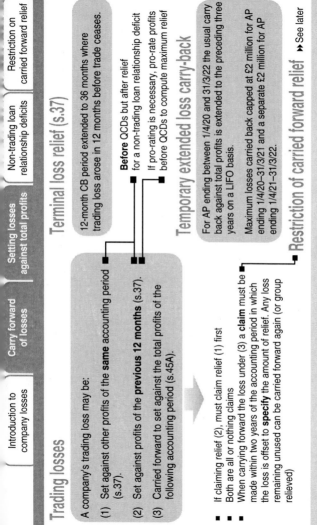

Non-trading loan relationship deficit (s.463B)

Set off against:

- Other profits of same AP
- Non-trading loan relationship income of previous 12 months
- Profits of group companies
- Total profits of the next AP

Can make partial claims

Given before:

- Relief for trading losses (under s.37);
- CB relief for non-trading loan relationships (under s.63B); and
- Relief for trading losses brought forward (under s.45A).

Priority of claims

Set current period losses against total profits in following order:

1. Deficits on NTLRs
2. Property business losses
3. Current period trading losses

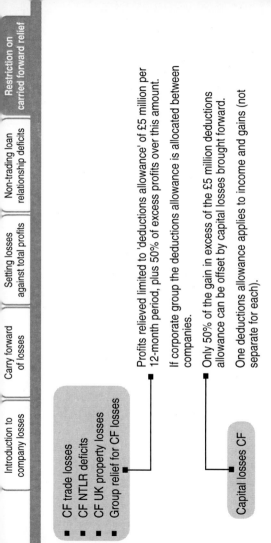

- CF trade losses
- CF NTLR deficits
- CF UK property losses
- Group relief for CF losses

Profits relieved limited to 'deductions allowance' of £5 million per 12-month period, plus 50% of excess profits over this amount.

If corporate group the deductions allowance is allocated between companies.

Capital losses CF

Only 50% of the gain in excess of the £5 million deductions allowance can be offset by capital losses brought forward.

One deductions allowance applies to income and gains (not separate for each).

Notes

22: Groups

You must be able to recognise the effect of being a member of a group on corporation tax payable and identify to which group companies a loss may be surrendered.

In addition, you must be able to recognise how chargeable gains can be reduced in a group.

Topic List

Group loss relief of current period losses

Group loss relief for carried forward losses

Definition of a chargeable gains group

Tax implications of gains groups

SSE for groups

Group relief group

One company must have a 75% effective interest in the other, or there must be a third company which has a 75% effective interest in both.

Group loss relief of current year losses

- Losses of one group company can be set against total profits of another
- Max = lower of available losses and available profits

Losses available to surrender

- Trading losses
- Deficits on non-trading loan relationships
- Excess qualifying charitable donations (QCDs)
- Excess property business losses

Note: Different rules for capital losses ▶▶ See later

Operation of relief

Set loss against TTP of claimant after CY and b/f reliefs but before c/b reliefs

- Group relief claim is normally made on the claimant company's tax return
- Claim relief within two years of end of claimant company's period of account

Group relief for carried-forward losses

- b/f trading losses, property losses and NTLR deficits can be surrendered through group relief
- Cannot be surrendered if company could use the loss against its own total profits in that period, but has not made a claim to use them
- Cannot claim group relief of carried-forward losses of another company if have any unused carried-forward losses of own
- Where claimant's profits exceed the deductions allowance, a max of 50% of remaining profits can be offset with b/f losses including those surrendered through group relief

Available profits

Available profits are TTP after deducting:

- Trading losses b/f
- CY trading losses whether claim or not
- NTLR b/f
- NTLR CY if claim made

But before deducting:

- Trading losses c/b
- NTLR c/b

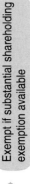

Group loss relief of current period losses	Group loss relief for carried forward losses	Definition of a chargeable gains group	Tax implications of gains groups	SSE for groups

Chargeable gains group

- Starts with principal company (must be included)
- Carries on down while 75% ordinary shareholding at each level
- Effective interest of principal company in subsidiary company > 50%

Intra-group transfers

No gain/loss arises when asset is transferred within a chargeable gains group.

- Ignore actual proceeds
- Deemed proceeds are:
  - Original cost; plus
  - Indexation to date of transfer (or December 2017 if earlier)
- Deemed proceeds become base cost for transferee company

Degrouping charge

- Transferee leaves group within six years of NGNL transfer
- Gain at transfer added to proceeds on sale of shares

Exempt if substantial shareholding exemption available

Election

- Can elect to transfer whole/part of chargeable gain/allowable loss to another member.
- Only 50% of gains in excess of deductions allowance may be offset by capital losses brought forward

Rollover relief

Members of a gains group may be treated as a single unit for rollover relief purposes.

Planning

Minimise group tax payable by transferring gain to company with capital losses.

SSE for groups

- In the TC exam will be told whether company is trading company for purposes of SSE
- Exemption does not apply to intra-group transfers
- Can combine group shareholdings

Ownership period of shares acquired via intra-group transfer = total time owned by group.

23: Value added tax

This chapter looks at some more complex areas of VAT in particular the consequences of group registration for VAT, the impact of partial exemption on input VAT recovery and the VAT issues relating to property transactions.

It also covers the capital goods scheme and the VAT issues of trading with non-EU states.

Topic List

Supplies

VAT groups

Partial exemption

Property transactions

Special schemes

Overseas aspects

1 Zero-rated supplies

Taxable at 0%
Eg, food, books and newspapers

2 Exempt supplies

Not taxable
Eg, insurance, education and health services

3 Standard-rated supplies

Taxable at 20%
All supplies which are not zero-rated, reduced rate or exempt

4 Reduced rate supplies

Taxable at 5%
Eg, fuel for domestic use, smoking cessation products and contraceptives

Alert! A person making only exempt supplies cannot recover VAT on inputs. Contrast this with a person making zero-rated (taxable supplies) who can recover VAT on inputs.

Supply of goods or services?

Important to differentiate as different rules may apply eg, place of supply rules.

Multiple (or combined) supply

Split into components. The appropriate VAT rate is applied to each component.

Single (or composite) supply

Cannot be split into components. One (the main) VAT rate applies.

Supply of goods

Treated as a supply of goods:

- Supply of any form of power, heat, etc
- Taking goods out of a business for non-business use

Supply of services

Treated as a supply of services:

- Goods hired to someone
- Goods lent to someone for use outside the business

Group registration

- Available to companies under **common control**, with a fixed establishment in the UK. Soletraders and partnerships can be included if they control all the members of the VAT group and have a business establishment in the UK.

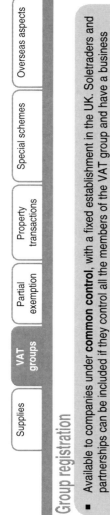

Representative member accounts for all VAT

Simplifies VAT accounting
No VAT on supplies between group members

All members jointly and severally liable for VAT

Reduces VAT accounting

Improves cash flow

- Companies only included in group if specific application made – not automatic
- Consider excluding companies making largely zero-rated supplies (which could claim monthly VAT repayments) and wholly exempt companies (to avoid partial exemption rules)

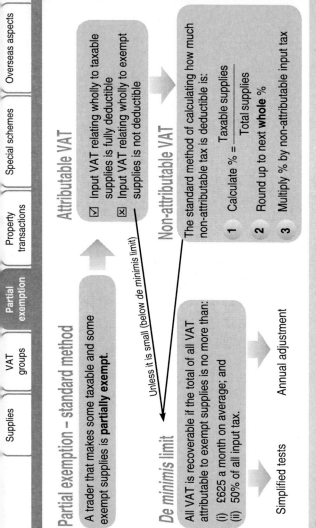

Partial exemption – standard method

A trader that makes some taxable and some exempt supplies is **partially exempt.**

Unless it is small (below *de minimis* limit)

Attributable VAT

☑ Input VAT relating wholly to taxable supplies is fully deductible

☒ Input VAT relating wholly to exempt supplies is not deductible

Non-attributable VAT

The standard method of calculating how much non-attributable tax is deductible is:

1 Calculate % = $\dfrac{\text{Taxable supplies}}{\text{Total supplies}}$

2 Round up to next **whole** %

3 Multiply % by non-attributable input tax

De minimis limit

All VAT is recoverable if the total of all VAT attributable to exempt supplies is no more than:

(i) £625 a month on average; and
(ii) 50% of all input tax.

Simplified tests

Annual adjustment

Simplified tests

Two simplified tests are available for partial exemption.

Test one

All VAT is recoverable if:

- Total input tax ≤ £625 per month on average; and
- Value of exempt supplies ≤ 50% of total supplies

Test two

All VAT is recoverable if:

- Total input tax less input tax directly attributable to taxable supplies ≤ £625 per month on average; and
- Value of exempt supplies ≤ 50% of total supplies

- If either test is met all input VAT for the VAT period is recoverable
- If fail both tests apply standard method to the VAT period

Annual adjustments

Apply simplified tests to VAT year:

- If meet either test all input VAT recoverable
- If fail both tests apply standard test to VAT year

Determine amount payable to/repayable from HMRC

- De minimis in one year means provisional recovery of in-year input tax in following year
- Annual adjustment only

Land and buildings

1. Land – exempt
2. **New** residential dwellings – zero-rated
3. Non-residential converted to residential – zero-rated
4. Freehold **new** commercial buildings – standard-rated
5. Other sales, most leases – exempt

Less than three years old

Subject to landlord's **option to tax** (**not** residential property)

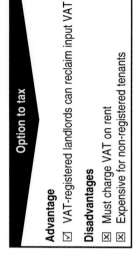

Option to tax

Advantage

☑ VAT-registered landlords can reclaim input VAT

Disadvantages

☒ Must charge VAT on rent
☒ Expensive for non-registered tenants

Capital goods scheme

Initial recovery of input tax on **certain capital goods** is adjusted to reflect variations in the taxable use of those goods.

Applies to:

- **Land and buildings** costing £250,000 or more – adjusted over ten years

- **Computers** costing £50,000 or more – adjusted over five years

- **Boats or aircraft** costing £50,000 or more – adjusted over five years

Adjustment each year:

- Difference between taxable use percentage for first year and taxable use percentage for current year

- × 1/10 (land) or 1/5 (computers, boats and aircraft)

On sale:

- Normal annual adjustment; **plus**

- Further adjustment for remaining years assuming taxable use of 0% (exempt sale) or 100% (taxable sale)

Flat rate scheme – limited cost traders

A limited cost business will use a flat rate percentage of 16.5% regardless of type of business.

A business is limited cost if amount spent on relevant goods (including VAT) is either:

- Less than 2% of VAT incl turnover
- Greater than 2% of VAT incl turnover but less than £1,000 per year

Supply of services

Takes place where:
- Supplier is, if customer not a relevant business person (B2C)
- Customer is, if customer is a relevant business person (B2B)

Reverse charge system if customer is UK VAT registered trader

Supplies of goods

Exports (between UK & non EU and GB & EU)
Exports of goods are zero-rated.

Imports (between UK & non EU and GB & EU)
Imports of goods are subject to VAT at the same rate as on a sale within the UK, at the point of entry into the UK. Postponed VAT accounting available to provide cashflow saving.

For supplies of goods between NI & GB
Supplier charges VAT and customer

24: Stamp taxes

You must understand the scope of the different stamp taxes, be able to calculate the relevant charges and understand when an exemption may be available.

Topic List

Stamp duty

Stamp duty reserve tax

Stamp duty land tax

Also known as an 'instrument'

Stamp duty

Paid by purchaser on transfers of shares by physical **document.**

1. 0.5% × consideration (only if > £1,000)
2. Round up to nearest £5

Stamp duty exemptions

- No chargeable consideration, eg, gifts
- On divorce
- Variations of Wills
- Certain intra-group share transfers
- Securities dealt on recognised growth markets

Administration of stamp duty

- Send document and stamp duty due to HMRC within 30 days of execution
- Late payment interest runs from end of 30 day period
- Penalty for late document:
  - < 12 months, 10% of duty, capped at £300
  - 12m – 24m, 20% of duty
  - > 24m, 30% of duty
    - Will be higher if deliberate failure
- No penalty charged if < £20

- Round down to nearest £5
- Only charged if ≥ £25

Stamp duty reserve tax

Paid on transfers of shares not caught by stamp duty, ie, paperless transactions.

1 0.5% × consideration

2 Do not round

SDRT exemptions

- No chargeable consideration, eg, gifts
- Securities dealt on recognised growth markets

Administration of SDRT

- Collected automatically via stockbrokers
- Due on:
  - 7th day of month following month of contract
  - 14 calendar days after trade date if can be made by CREST
- Penalties for failure to make return and late payment – common penalty regime

Stamp duty land tax

Payable by purchaser on land transactions eg:

- Transfer of freehold land
- Assignment of lease
- Grant of lease

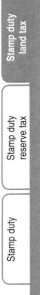

Also charged on lease premium + net present value (NPV) of rent

Premium: SDLT charged under normal rates in table below

NPV:

- Residential: 1% on excess over £125,000
- Non-residential: 1% between £150,000 and £5m
  2% on excess over £5m

Rate (%)	Residential	Rate (%)	Non-residential
0	£Nil – £125,000	0	£Nil – £150,000
2	£125,001 – £250,000	2	£150,001 – £250,000
5	£250,001 – £925,000	5	£250,001 and over
10	£925,001 – £1,500,000		
12	£1,500,001 and over		

Payable on amount that falls in each bracket

Two periods of temporary relief to SDLT for residential properties:

- 8/7/20–30/6/21; and
- 1/7/21–30/9/21

See Hardmans for details.

Additional 3% if cost > £40,000 and already owns residential property (unless replacement main residence).

Relief for first time buyers for consideration up to £500,000. Rates are 0% on first £300,000 with 5% on any excess. No relief if consideration > £500,000.

SDLT exemptions

- No chargeable consideration, eg, gifts
- On divorce
- Variations of Wills
- Transfer of land between members of 75% group ── Unless:
  - Arrangements
  - Not for *bona fide* commercial purposes

SDLT administration

- File land transaction form (even if no SDLT payable)
- Within 14 days of transaction
- Also pay tax within 14 days of transaction
- Late payment interest from end of 14 day period to day before SDLT paid
- Penalties for late filing:
  - Up to three months late: £100 automatic penalty
  - Over three months late: £200 automatic penalty
  - Over one year late: tax geared penalty up to amount of SDLT payable